MAKE MONEY WRITING BOOKS: Proven Profit-Making Strategies for Authors

For additional printed copies or bulk discounts use Order Form at end of this book or contact:

**Robert W. Lucas Enterprises
1555 Pinehurst Drive
Casselberry, FL 32718-0487 USA
407-695-5535
http://www.robertwlucas.com**

What People Are Saying About *Make Money Writing Books*

In *Make Money Writing Books*, Bob Lucas has mined all the wisdom and experience of his nearly 20 years as a financially successful author and trainer and compressed them into a compact, comprehensive publication. Chock full of superb suggestions for marketing, promotion, branding and more, it is an invaluable resource for anyone wishing to enjoy monetary gain from the hard and exhilarating work of creating books.
Chris Angermann, President, Florida Authors and Publishers Association

What a gift to aspiring authors! Bob's book offers a blueprint for writing, publishing, and marketing your first book. Use his guidance and watch your success as an author build. Thank you, Bob, for taking the lead in creating what will surely be the foundation for many authors.
Elaine Beich, ebb associates, inc, Author, The Business of Consulting and Editor, The ASTD Leadership Handbook

If you've written a book, good for you! But, if it's not selling, you need Bob Lucas on your side. If you want to write a book, but don't know how to start, you need to read Bob Lucas. If you feel there ought to be more to life than writing a book, you should listen to the ideas Bob Lucas has. *Make Money Writing* is about making money from your writing, but it's also about so much more. By following the outlines and advice in this book, you'll make yourself into the professional author you want to be with the following you deserve.
Chrissy Jackson, President, Chrissy Jackson & Associates, Inc. www.Chrissy-Jackson.com

I've always marveled at Bob Lucas' ability to write so many books of practical advice (in the 30s now) and do them all so well. This one is a must, and a keeper, for any writer ... especially a new one hoping to get published. My first book (Training With a Beat) came out in 2000. Looking back on it, the process was more difficult than it needed to be. If only Making Money Writing Books was available then. With chapters on how to be a good writer, avoiding writer's block, getting yourself known, what a publisher will and won't do, promoting yourself within your industry, marketing your book, and whether to self or publishing house publish, Bob's advice is solid throughout. It's a succinct guide through the must-knows of the writing/publishing maze.
Lenn Millbower, the Learnertainment Trainer

You may be a great writer, but if people don't know how to find you it won't matter. Developing an author platform is one key to making money writing that will lead to exposure and promotion for you and your books. By personally "branding" yourself as an expert and author, you increase opportunities to sell more books and generate additional income streams through personal appearances and product lines based on your brand. In Make Money Writing Books, Robert W Lucas offers many valuable ideas for doing all of this and more. He also provides helpful web links to people and organizations that can assist in your writing and marketing efforts. Definitely a useful resource for anyone who writes books or is thinking of doing so.
Rik Feeney / Author: Writing Books for Fun, Fame and Fortune!

I've read lots of books on the writing and marketing process. I was the most impressed with the information, resources, and

ideas presented in this one. I can't imagine any author, especially first time ones, not having access to this knowledge about book publishing and marketing; especially marketing!
Zame Khan, Training Design Expert

In his book Bob Lucas has laid out detailed insider steps and strategies to help authors be successful once they have written their masterpiece. He lays out what he has learned over the years in how to market books whether working with a publishing house or self-publishing. He also has gone the extra step and has provided readers with "worksheets" to help them use these strategies and success steps in their own situation. This is a book where everyone can get ideas to help them be more successful!
Steve Tanzer, ECC, LCS, IATAN

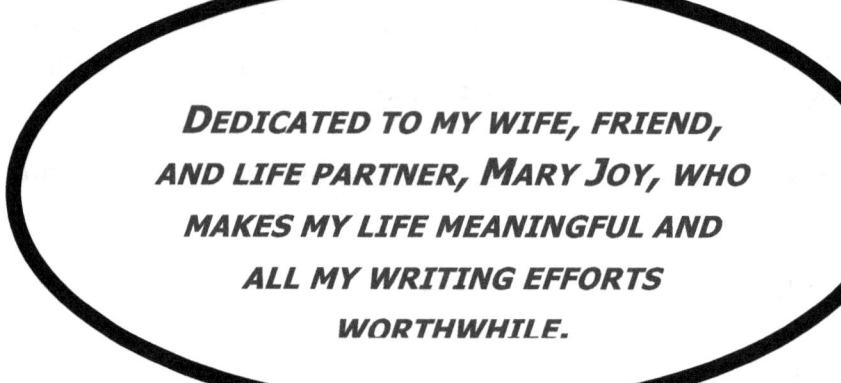

Dedicated to my wife, friend, and life partner, Mary Joy, who makes my life meaningful and all my writing efforts worthwhile.

Special thanks for the support and expertise from my friends and colleagues listed below who made my goal of publishing this book a reality.

Chris Angermann (graphic and publishing guidance)
Elaine Beich (review and feedback)
Rik Feeney (self-publishing suggestions and advice)
Chrissy Jackson (review and feedback)
Sharon Massen (editorial guidance and services)
Joleene Naylor (graphic and cover design guidance)

ABOUT THE AUTHOR

Bob Lucas is the Principal at *Robert W. Lucas Enterprises*, an internationally-known author and learning and performance expert who specializes in workplace performance-based training and consulting services. He has four decades of experience in human resources development, management, and customer service in a variety of organizational environments. Bob has served on various non-profit boards where he has been President of the Central Florida Chapter of the Association for Talent Development (formerly the American Society for Training and Development) twice and Chair of Leadership Seminole in Seminole County, Florida and served on the board for the Florida Authors and Publishers Association (FAPA).

Listed in *Who's Who in the World, Who's Who in America, and Who's Who in the South & Southeast, Bob* is also an avid writer. He has the top selling customer service textbook in the United States and has written and contributed to 32 books and hundreds of training leader guides and support materials for several training videos. He has also been a contributing author for the *Annual: Developing Human Resources* series by Pfeiffer & Company since 1992 and several other compilation works by various publishers.

Bob earned a Bachelor of Science degree in Law Enforcement from the University of Maryland, an M.A degree with a focus in Human Resources Development from George Mason University in Fairfax, Virginia, and a second M.A. degree in Management and Leadership from Webster University in Orlando, Florida.

CONTACT BOB LUCAS

Phone: +1-407-695-5535 (United States)
E-Mail: blucas@robertwlucas.com
Website: http://www.robertwlucas.com

Like Bob at:
http://www.facebook.com/robertwlucasenterprises
Non-Fiction Writing Blog:
http://www.robertwlucas.com/wordpress
Creative Training Blog:
http://www.thecreativetrainer.com
Customer Service Blog:
http://customerserviceskillsbook.com

MAKE MONEY WRITING BOOKS:
Proven Profit-Making Strategies for Authors

Robert W. Lucas
Principal, Robert W. Lucas Enterprises
www.robertwlucas.com

Copyright © 2015 by Robert W. Lucas.

Published by Success Skills Press
1555 Pinehurst Drive
Casselberry, Florida 32707 USA

All rights reserved. Printed in the United States of America. Except as permitted under the United States Copyright Law of 1976, no part of this publication may be reproduced or distributed in any form or by any means, electronic or mechanical, including photocopying, recording or otherwise, or stored in a database or retrieval system, without the prior written permission of the copyright owner.

Distributed by Robert W. Lucas Enterprises

ISBN-10: 1-939884-00-4
ISBN-13: 978-1-939884-00-8
Library of Congress Control Number: 2013903821

The content of this book contains the sole opinions of the author based on his experience and knowledge as a published author, along with references to others, and should be treated as such. All attempts have been made to ensure that all information, websites, and references contained in this book are correct and accurate at the time of publication. **The content is provided for informational purposes. Neither the author nor the publisher make any warranties or representations related to content, nor do they assume any liability for errors, omissions, or inaccuracies of subject matter contained herein or for damages suffered as a result of content application.** Any incorrect attributions in the book are inadvertent and will be corrected in future editions if notifications are made to the publisher.

This publication is designed to provide accurate and authoritative information in regard to the subject matter covered. It is sold with the understanding that neither the author nor the publisher is engaged in rendering legal, accounting, securities trading, or other professional services. If legal advice or other expert assistance is required, the services of a competent professional person should be sought.

From a Declaration of Principles Jointly Adopted by a Committee of the American Bar Association and a Committee of Publishers and Associations.

Editorial: Sharon Massen
Cover photos by Maridav, Scanrail & Can Stock Photo Inc.
Cover Design by Joleene Naylor

CONTENTS

What Others Are Saying About Make Money Writing Books

Acknowledgements

About the Author

Contact Bob Lucas

Table of Contents

INTRODUCTION 1

CHAPTER I: WRITING SUCCESS STRATEGIES . 7

Lesson 1 – There is no ONE Secret to Writing Success! . . . 8

Lesson 2 – Effective Writing Must Come from the Heart . . 9

Lesson 3 – You Must Know Yourself Well 12

Lesson 4 – There is No Substitute for Sound Research . . . 15

Lesson 5 – You Must Find Your Own Voice 16

Lesson 6 – Break Your Writing Into Chunks 18

Lesson 7 – Show Up for the Game 20

Lesson 8 – Selling is the Author's Responsibility 22

Lesson 9 –Additional Income Streams are Crucial to Authors 24

Lesson 10 – Never Pay for Something You Can Get Otherwise 27

PLANNING WORKSHEET 30

CHAPTER II: BECOME A KNOWN ENTITY 33

DEMONSTRATE CREDIBILITY 36

- Enter Writing Contests 38

- Seek Book Reviews 39

- Arrange Local Media Interviews 40

GAIN NAME RECOGNITION 42

- Find Ways to Stay in the Forefront. 42

- Reinforce or Remind 43

- Share Links with Other Sites 45

BECOME AN ASSET 45

- Volunteer 46

- Speak or Train Others 47

- Deliver Podcasts 52

- Conduct Webinars 55

- Coach or Mentor 56

- Create Tip or Fact Sheets 59

- Conduct Original Research 59

- Offer Sponsorships 60

JOIN WRITERS GROUPS 61

PLANNING WORKSHEET 62

CHAPTER III: PROMOTE YOURSELF 63

REPRESENT YOUR BOOKS, PRODUCTS AND SERVICES PROFESSIONALLY 64

- Create a Press Release 66

- Develop a Press/Media Kit. 67

- Network with Others and Share Ideas 68

- Attend Conferences and Professional Development Events 70

- Hold Neighborhood Book Signings 71

- Exhibit at Professional Trade Shows 72

- Go to Book Fairs 73

- Set Up Autograph Events 75

- Submit for Book Awards .76

ADVERTISE 79

- Pay-Per-Click Advertising 80

- Affiliate Advertising 81

GET ASSISTANCE 83

- Tap Into Your Network 83

- Search for Online Resources 84

- Form Alliances with Other Authors and Writers 86

PLANNING WORKSHEET 87

CHAPTER IV: CREATE MARKETING MATERIALS 89

DEVELOP PRINTED MARKETING MATERIALS 89

- Professional Business Cards 92

- Product Brochures 95

- Book/Product Flyers 96
- Postcards 99
- Incentives/Giveaways 100
- Magnetic Signs 102

PLANNING WORKSHEET 103

CHAPTER V: CREATE AN ONLINE PRESENCE . 105

DEVELOP A WEBSITE 105

- Web Hosting 106
- Website Design 108
- Naming Your Website 111
- Website Content 115

ARTICLES 120

BLOG 122

- Create Your Own Blog 122
- Guest Blog 125
- Monetize Your Blog 126
- *Pay-per-click ads* 126

- *Pay-per Action ads* 127

- *Pay-per-impression ads* 127

SOCIAL MEDIA 128

- LinkedIn 129

- Facebook 129

- Twitter 130

- Pinterest 130

SIGNATURE LINE ON EMAIL MESSAGES 132

PLANNING WORKSHEET 134

CHAPTER VI: DEVELOP PRODUCTS 135

WRITE ARTICLES 135

WRITE AN EBOOK 136

CREATE COMPLEMENTARY PRODUCTS 140

- Fiction Book Products 141

- Non-Fiction Book Products 142

PLANNING WORKSHEET 144

CHAPTER VII: WHAT TO DO NEXT 145

PERSONAL ACTION PLAN 149

OTHER BOOKS BY ROBERT W. LUCAS 153

ABOUT ROBERT W. LUCAS ENTERPRISES 155

ADDITIONAL RESOURCES 157

Books and Publications 157

Organizations and Associations 161

REQUEST FOR REVIEWS 163

BOOK ORDER FORMS

"Success is not the key to happiness. Happiness is the key to success. If you love what you are doing, you will be successful."
Albert Schweitzer

INTRODUCTION

The world is full of people fed up with just scraping by financially and looking for ways to express themselves creatively, make money, improve their life, supplement their income, and build a better retirement. Isn't that why you bought this book? Why shouldn't you take advantage of this trend and benefit from your own knowledge, skill, or passion?

In these unsteady times where an organization that you might be part of is experiencing downsizing, rightsizing or capsizing as a norm, or in a situation where you are dependent on clients or others to provide income for your personal and family support, wouldn't it be nice to have a safety net that *you* control? This is possible for those who create books and associated useful products and services that are placed into the marketplace. Such products can potentially earn a stream of income while you sleep.

For example, imagine that you wrote a short book, such as the one you are reading, and turned it into an eBook along with small print runs of paper copies for back-of-the-room sales (you will read about these in this book). Now assume that you took 3 to 4 weeks to write and edit your book, as I did with this one, and then priced your eBook at $2.99 on Amazon or some other Web distribution site. If you sold only 50 to 100 books a month, you would make approximately $100 to $200 dollars a month. Multiply that by twelve months and you are making $1,200 to $2,400 a year on a single title. Take your imagination further and assume that you could write six such books a year (one every two months) and they all sold equally as well. That is around $7,200 to $15,000 a year, and you don't have to do anything else to those books! And, that is only for the eBook versions. Spend a bit of money from revenues generated from your electronic versions and have printed copies made and distributed through a service such as Lightning Source (http://www.lightningsource.com) or CreateSpace (http://www.createspace.com). You could also sell the books on your own website or others, via mail and in the back of the room if you speak to groups, thus increasing your revenue stream.

I assume that if you are reading this book, you have already decided to move forward with your own writing project(s) and are now looking for ways to capitalize on your efforts. You likely want to know the secrets of successful writers and how they make money at the art of writing books. In this book, I share some productive and profitable strategies that have worked for me as an author for over three decades and self-publisher. Since 1994, thirty-two of my books have been published by major publishers and associations (e.g. Irwin, McGraw-Hill, American Management Association [AMA], Jossey-

Bass/Pfeiffer, and the Association for Talent Development [ATD]). I have also self-published books and professional training materials for over four decades. Several of these books have been translated in India, Italy and Korea.

Many authors approach writing as drudgery or another task that they must complete. Those people typically fail. Like any other successful venture, before you start writing you have to be confident that what you have to say is important and that you can do so in a professional, positive and interesting manner. You also have to decide why you are writing early in the process if you plan to be successful. As an author, you will spend many hours in front of a computer or notepad developing your masterpiece, editing and re-editing. For that reason, it is crucial that you decide what you hope to gain from all your effort. Many writers do it for fame, fortune, self-satisfaction, or to leave a legacy for their heirs. You have to figure out what your motivation is and not lose sight of that when, not if, writer's block occurs and you feel stymied in putting words to paper. Once you have a vision, you are on your way to creating a vehicle that can earn you a steady stream of residual and passive income into your future years and possibly even make you rich.

As you read through *Make Money Writing Books*, you are going to find proven techniques and strategies that I have used for over four decades. These techniques and strategies have served me well in my professional career working for companies, as the owner of an online business, and as a consultant. During that time, I have also written hundreds of articles and dozens of books and other published materials, including the current best-selling customer service textbook in the United States - *Customer Service Skills for Success* with McGraw-Hill Publishing. The royalties from that book alone have allowed me and my family to live comfortably, travel around the United States and the world regularly, and take one or two cruises and other vacations a year for over a decade.

In *Make Money Writing Books: Proven Profit Making Strategies for Authors* you will read about:

- *Writing Success Strategies.* These are based on lessons that I have learned in writing books for the past twenty years.

- *Becoming a Known Entity.* To sell your books, products, and services, you must find ways to gain name and face recognition. You want to be known as the "go to" person for your specialty or genre. You will read about ways to help accomplish this in these pages.

- *Promoting Yourself.* A major part of becoming known and gaining exposure for your books, products, and services is to find ways to get the word out about what you do. I have added a chapter with some simple, free or inexpensive ways to accomplish this later in the book.

- *Creating Marketing Materials.* There are many types of marketing materials that you might consider as a way to sharing information about yourself and your books, products, and services. One chapter in this book addresses some proven strategies for helping to market yourself and what you offer.

- *Creating an Online Presence.* Technology has made information sharing a relatively simple and crucial part of your book marketing strategy. You will read about some simple ways to help spread the word about your books online.

- *Developing Products.* One goal of successful authors and professionals is to stay in the forefront of the minds of readers. A simple way of aiding this effort is to have "stuff" to give people. In the last chapter of the book, I have shared some strategies that have served me well over the years.

Once you finish reading the book, I'd love to hear your feedback and answer any questions that you have. You can contact me by emailing info@robertwlucas.com or through my website http://www.robertwlucas.com. My website also has additional useful information along with hundreds of articles and links to the blogs that I author on non-fiction writing, customer service, and creative training.

As you will find as an author, reviews of your work are important factors in your success. I would appreciate your visiting http://www.amazon.com to write a review on this book.

Happy and Profitable Writing,

Bob Lucas
http://www.robertwlucas.com

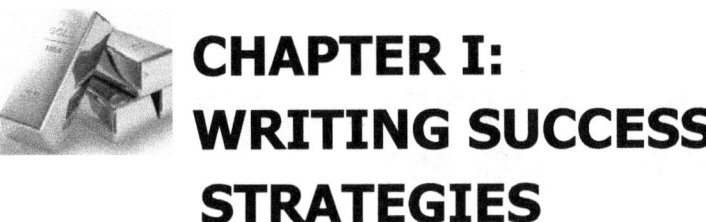

CHAPTER I: WRITING SUCCESS STRATEGIES

"Life doesn't come with an instruction manual."
Scott Westerfeld

Sure things typically do not exist in life. As humans we are fallible and not perfect. We all make mistakes, but hopefully we learn from our blunders and those made by others. The little "lessons" that we experience throughout our lives can serve as a blueprint for future success if we pay attention and do not keep repeating our mistakes.

To help you on your road to making more money from your endeavors, I want to share ten of the lessons that I've learned along the way as an author and writer. I assume that you have already written, are writing, or will soon start working on a book that is important to you. My hope is that my life experiences will aid you in conducting activities related to effectively developing and marketing them, branding yourself, and making more money.

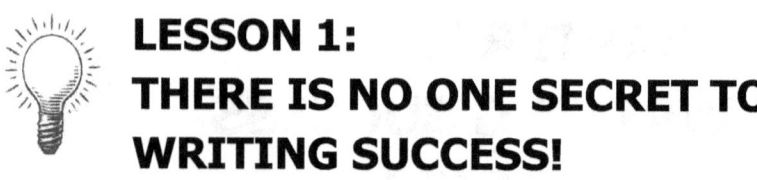
LESSON 1: THERE IS NO ONE SECRET TO WRITING SUCCESS!

I could have titled this book "THE Secret to Making Money as a Writer," but that would be misleading, and I want to you have realistic expectations about potential outcomes from your writing efforts.

One thing that I have learned as a writer and author for over two decades is that there is no "one" secret to success. In fact, success for one person does not define the same for someone else. Each of us must set a goal and work toward gaining the knowledge that will help us attain that individually. Since we each have different views on what success entails, you have to decide on your own where you would like your writing efforts to take you.

The *Resources* section of this book lists several excellent sources of information on how to get your books and materials published. They can also help in the crucial step of establishing yourself as an expert and effectively marketing your books and/or related services.

Writing and publishing groups are another great place to find books, articles, and additional resources on the writing and publishing process. If you do an Internet search you will find numerous professional groups dedicated to helping writers and self-publishers succeed. Many of those organizations may be in your geographic area. You will also find a listing of some organizations and associations, such as the ones I have listed at the end of this book and have found useful over the years.

LESSON 2:
EFFECTIVE WRITING MUST COME FROM THE HEART

A second "ah-ha" for me as an author was that *writing must come from the heart* if being successful at it is your goal. Writing can be hard work and quite honestly, many people do not have the initiative, ability, or true desire to put in the hours required to develop and edit material and effectively promote what they write.

You must also research the publishing process and learn the basics of how books and articles become printed materials and how they are marketed and distributed afterwards. You will be an intricate part of those phases of the process.

Having an idea or specific topic knowledge is only the first step in your journey to write a book, article, or other publication. It does not matter whether you plan to write fiction or non-fiction books, you have to do your homework by learning the mechanics of writing (*e.g.* spelling, grammar, syntax, and punctuation). Granted there are technology-based tools (*e.g.* spelling and grammar checkers) that can help offset shortcomings in some of these areas. But they are not infallible and cannot be depended upon to substitute for your ability to script an effective message. Ultimately, you should invest in hiring editors to review what you have written in order to make sure that it is in a professional format and is the best that it can be.

There are typically three types of editors that you should consider for your project:
- *Developmental editor.* These people look at the entire scope of the project and offer suggestions on reformatting, moving material to different points in the book, changes, additions, and

deletions. Keep in mind that you, not they, are the subject matter expert on your content and that you must make final decisions on their recommended changes. Their job is to help you mold the product into a valuable, sellable one.

- *Copy editor.* These professionals are the ones who read through what you have written in an effort to catch incorrect, grammar, punctuation, syntax and other elements that are incorrect.

- *Proofreader.* After everyone else has done their job, these editors will read through multiple times in an effort to catch any errors, omissions and elements that need revision. I recommend that after they finish, you pass along copies to friends, relatives, peers, and members of any critique groups to which you belong and ask that they also review for possible errors and omissions.

One thing that I have learned after writing thirty-three books with major publishers is that even with all this effort, there is always something that gets overlooked. Keep in mind that it is your name on the front of the publication. Therefore, it is in your best interests to go through one more time after all the experts, friends and software have worked their magic to ensure that anything that might be wrong can be caught before publication.

Once you have created your books, you must put the same passion into marketing them as you did writing. That is the only way to make money. Otherwise, they are printed books sitting in your garage or an eBook that only a few people ever read.

LESSON 3:
YOU MUST KNOW YOURSELF WELL

Writing is for the most part a solitary activity with you and your computer or notepad sitting alone for hours and days on end. On the other hand, effective marketing requires you to blend solitary efforts (*e.g.* sending out news releases, creating media kits, writing blogs or developing marketing materials) with contact events (*e.g.* participating in media interviews, giving presentations, and networking at group events).

If you are an extroverted person, writing can be a painful process, and you will need to compensate by building "people" time into your writing schedule. That means taking breaks to go to lunch with friends, family, or colleagues to provide a mental break. During those breaks you can certainly discuss what you are working on and solicit ideas and feedback, but you should also focus on other non-writing ideas and subjects to help stimulate your brain neurons and exercise other parts of your brain. These are also excellent opportunities to promote your books, share marketing materials, and educate others about what you do.

If you tend to be a more introverted person, you may have to force yourself out into the world with others periodically so that you have a periodic change of venue, get some fresh air and exercise the body while bouncing ideas off others. All of these actions are important in making you the best that you can be when writing. Additionally, the contacts you make during these networking events will likely provide valuable resources when the time comes to edit and market your final product.

One thing I have found extraordinarily helpful over my writing career, and in life, has been to complete self-assessment instruments or surveys that helped me understand myself and others and my behavioral preferences a little better. These self-scored tools can provide insights and validate understanding about the way you think and act in different situations and environments.

Some of the more popular surveys available today are the Myers-Briggs Type Indicator and the Personal Profile System (DiSC). These products can be purchased online from various distributors. Recognizing what makes you think and act in a certain manner and whether you prefer people, tasks, or a combination can provide you with the mental tools to help determine in what ways you can best focus your writing talents and become proficient at written communication.

LESSON 4:
THERE IS NO SUBSTITUTE FOR SOUND RESEARCH

Just like learning a language, how to play a musical instrument, or master any sport, there is no getting around the fact that you must put in the hours required to learn the discipline or activity and practice in order to get better at it. The same is true with writing. It does not make a difference whether you are developing characters and a plot or defining a concept or process; if you are going to produce fiction or non-fiction content that others will pay for, read, and come back for more in future books, you must spend time researching. This means hours of scanning bookshelves, libraries, the Internet, and other sources for current data, facts, and information related to your topic. You also have to check out the competition to ensure that your material is not only written in a format that readers expect but also is unique and interesting, or at least does not simply mimic what others have written.

As part of the writing and publication process, you should be researching the best practices for branding yourself and creating a marketing strategy. Use the content of this book as a starting point if you have not already begun your marketing strategy.

LESSON 5: YOU MUST FIND YOUR OWN VOICE

Each writer has a message that she or he wants to communicate to readers. He or she must also find his or her own unique approach to sharing ideas, stories, and information with readers in a manner that captures and holds attention. This is sometimes referred to as the author's *voice* and means nothing more than your style of writing. This is what separates the best-selling authors and writers from the wannabees.

If you are writing fiction, think of books you have read in the past that have captivated your attention. The ones that kept you hanging on every word. The ones that you were willing to stay up all night and miss meals for or otherwise not want to put the book down so that you could get to the next page to find out what happens. What made those books different from others you had read that could not pull you in like that? Try to capture the same essence in your own writing style. Additionally, when you are creating characters for a non-fiction work, they need to be new, interesting, memorable, and "speak" to readers rather than being copies of those found in other written material or media.

Should you prefer to write non-fiction, decide what you will provide to readers in the form of information. Speak with authority and confidence. Focus on a format that will make it meaningful and valuable to readers. Words are not enough. You must also consider other aspects that will hold attention while adding to the theme of the topic. This might include elements such as:

- Activities.
- Subject-related cartoons.
- Sidebars of information (*e.g.* bulleted lists, resources, or other complimentary information).
- Photos that relate to the written words.
- Graphs or other visual content that help people picture what you are explaining in the words.

Visual aspects can aid comprehension for many people who tend to best assimilate information by picturing it in their mind. Just do not go overboard with images and graphics that might detract from your written message. This is true in your books and in your marketing materials. Anything you use should have a purpose and point directly to your overall message.

LESSON 6:
BREAK YOUR WRITING INTO CHUNKS

If you must eat an elephant, it is best to do it one bite at a time! What that means is that, rather than tackling an entire writing project and plugging through, create a writing action plan and schedule, and then work on small sections over a period of time. Similarly, rather than tackling all your marketing initiatives at once, space your research, development of materials, and initiatives to get the word out into chunks. Try doing one activity a day to market yourself and your books until you feel comfortable increasing the effort.

For example, rather than saying, "I am going to write until I am tired" or "I am going to write two chapters today," plan to write for an hour or identify a reasonable number of pages or timeframe that you will write before taking a break or quitting for the day. This approach keeps your mind alert, keeps you focused and will not burn you out on the project or the writing in general. It also helps prevent you from getting blood clots in your legs from sitting too long...always get up periodically and walk around for five to ten minutes throughout your day.

This strategy should also be employed if you are researching content for your work. Rather than spending eight hours searching the Internet for articles, information and ideas, set aside a short block of time. Once you decide on a topic, start gathering material over a period of time as you come across things that might add value to what you plan to write. Keep articles and web links written down and placed in a folder on your computer or in a manila folder. Capturing your thoughts can also be done with writing software designed for authors such as Scrivener (http://www.literatureandlatte.com/scrivener). The latter allows you to click and drag research domain names into a research folder in the software to access later and to pin thoughts on an electronic corkboard for future reference.

LESSON 7: SHOW UP FOR THE GAME

Imagine a sports team scheduled for a playoff game. The team does all the pre-work and the getting ready for the big event through conditioning and hard play. Then on the day of the event their star player decides not to show up. That would be akin to your doing all your project research, developing an outline for content, gathering your materials together, and then deciding you were not in the mood to write your article or book.

Writing is not a glamorous activity. Like any job, there will be times when you want to "call in sick" and take the day off. That is okay, as long as you do not make that a habit and spend more days out sick than at work. In fact, it is a good thing to get out and take a break periodically in order to refresh yourself mentally and physically. Just remember that if you do not write; the work will never get into print. By continually avoiding writing, you may even develop writer's block and start to question your own ability or motivation to get the material done at all.

Set up a schedule for writing and stick with it unless a true emergency arises. If you are a morning person and have more energy and mental focus in the early part of the day, write then. On the other hand, if you peak later in the day, select that time period for your creative efforts. Whatever works best for you, identify it and stay with it. Pretty soon, you will find the words and ideas flowing onto paper as you exercise your brain and paint images or create useful strategies in writing.

Once you are ready to market your book(s), create a written plan of what activities you plan to conduct, dates when you will do them, resources required, other people who might be involved, costs, and any other factor you can think of. If you are good at developing spreadsheets, create one with these headings and track your efforts daily, weekly, and monthly. This provides a visual record of your progress, helps identify gaps, and can serve as a motivator as you see progress made. The key is to do something every day to brand and market yourself and your books. Otherwise, your revenue will not increase.

LESSON 8:
SELLING IS THE AUTHOR'S RESPONSIBILITY

One thing I did not understand when I started writing for major book publishers in 1994 is that a publisher typically takes care of functions such as getting the ISBN (the coded number that appears on the back of every book), the product development, editing, cover and layout design, and all the technical sides of the printing and publishing of a book. Once the book is in print, the publisher may also handles basic logistic and marketing tasks such as warehousing, sending out news releases and review copies, and listing the book in its catalog and/or on their website and on the Amazon and Barnes & Noble websites. Most additional marketing and selling of the book rests pretty much with the author.

Realize that if you self-publish, all these production and distribution functions AND the marketing and selling are your responsibility. For this reason, I have used major publishers for all my books, until this one. That was because I was simultaneously running a consulting business, an online retail store, volunteering on several non-profit boards concurrently, and speaking around the country in addition to writing all my books. Plus, I was trying to have some semblance of a normal family life. As you can imagine, all this was quite a stretch. Fortunately, I have a tolerant and wonderful spouse who not only supported me, but also assisted in editing many of my works.

A few years ago, I decided to focus my efforts primarily on writing and promoting my books and closed down my two companies. This is why the book you are reading exists today. I got tired of doing all the creative aspects of the content and development and then having a publishing company handle the physical sides of the publishing process, along with some minor aspects of marketing. In exchange they were getting at least 85 percent of the book royalties. I figured that if I am going to take on a major share of the post-production marketing, I would do it all and keep more profit for me.

Of course you have to make your own decision about what is best for you. Going the route of using major publishing houses may work for you depending on your genre and how prolific and successful you are. It has certainly provided me with a comfortable income over the years. Still, at this point in my life I want to branch out and take advantage of the ease of use with electronic technology to see how I might develop a new line of products. I also enjoy the challenge of learning new skills related to self-publishing and starting a new venture that has the potential to generate a significant amount of residual and passive income in the future.

LESSON 9: ADDITIONAL INCOME STREAMS ARE CRUCIAL TO AUTHORS

Speaking of residual and passive income, I figured out years ago that developing a residual stream of extra money coming in each year is a smart approach. In today's economy and changing world, you cannot depend on others to take care of you and your family. The eras of spending 20 or 30 years with a firm and receiving lifetime retirement benefits later are mostly a relic of the past. Today, most people need multiple strategies for providing income and security before and after retirement. That is where writing comes in as a way to create products that earn you money while you sleep.

It is true that most writers do not get rich. Those lucky enough to sell articles to major magazines, have best-selling books, movie scripts adapted from their books, and product lines created from their book theme are few and far between when you look at how many people write articles and books. However, with people looking for a variety of entertainment sources, information that will improve their lives, and materials that can be accessed when they want it; writing articles and books provides a viable option for revenue generation.

Writing books is a lot simpler and cheaper than ever before. This is true primarily because of the ease of development on a computer and a myriad of ways to market and sell them on the Internet. Also, the simplicity and lower cost of doing Print on Demand (POD) publishing, where anyone can produce small quantities of books, provides a significant cost savings tool. That is because instead of having to do print runs of 1,000-5,000, as was required to be cost effective in past years, you can print ten or more books cheaply as they are needed.

Once you have a successful book, you might also consider developing a line of products associated with your successful books. Think of spin off materials you have seen in the past for books that have been turned into movie scripts like *Star Wars, Indiana Jones, Harry Potter,* and others. Everything from cups, mouse pads, towels and t-shirts carry the name and familiar logos of these titles. Look what authors such as Mark Victor Hansen and Jack Canfield have done in developing a product line for their series *Chicken Soup for the Soul.* See the following website for an example of just such easy marketing: (http://www.chickensoup.com/cs.asp?cid=licensed_products).

 The key in applying all of the strategies that you just read is for you to give advance thought to what and how you want to write and then follow a pre-planned strategy.

LESSON 10: NEVER PAY FOR SOMETHING YOU CAN GET OTHERWISE

A question I often hear from new authors and writers is "How much does writing and publishing a book cost?" The answer is that "it varies."

With electronic technology, if you have a computer and know how to use it, you can get a lot of the material and information you need, and you already have most of the tools required for writing and publishing a book. The Internet is a gold mine of information and resources for writers and self-publishers. A lot of free material and instructions needed to perform many of the functions you will need to address during the process is available on various websites.

One thing that I strongly recommend is that you never pay for something you can get otherwise. Most people have knowledge and skills that others need and want. If you need a service (*e.g.* ghostwriting, word processing, transcription, editing, graphic and cover design, or printing) that you do not know how to do, barter for it with services you can provide. You might also trade something you have for what you need.

The last thing you should do is to go into heavy debt, or spend money you have not made from your writing. Never spend anticipated money. Wait until the royalty check has cleared the bank or funds become available from sales before counting on such income.

Many first time authors fall prey to vendors who charge high prices and require up-front payments. For example, some vanity presses charge a fee to publish and distribute your books. Avoid such arrangements and seek reputable book printers and publishers who are more author-friendly. Ask other writers (e.g. at professional meetings, seminars, or online chat sites) for advice and recommendations before striking out on your own. Also check with the Better Business Bureau or other such agencies before handing over money to companies and individuals you do not know personally. Also, never take out large loans or mortgages to fund your writing career. There are other ways to generate cash shown in this book and other sources that can help you determine a more stable fiscal approach to getting your name in print. Depending on your topic, consider the growing trend of checking with crowdsourcing websites.

Do your research online to identify potential resources or bartering venues. Additionally, by networking with others, you can identify people who have the talents and resources that you need.

As you will read later, get out from behind your computer and meet people at professional meetings, in writers groups, in social settings, at religious gatherings and just about anywhere you may be, even while shopping. Always have a professional looking business card handy and talk about your project without giving away plots or too much information, and while using some common sense. You will be amazed how many people will respond.

PLANNING WORKSHEET

Before you go further in the book, take some time to reflect on the following questions and jot capture your responses on a sheet of paper or in an electronic file. Use this as a planning sheet for preparing to generate revenue from your books.

1. How can the lessons I just read about help me plan a strategy for becoming a more successful author?

2. What other lessons have I already learned that might help me become a better author who generates a steady stream of income?

3. Whom do I know who might share other pertinent lessons as an author?

4. What local groups might help me become a better known and compensated author?

5. What challenges do I face in becoming a known and successful author?

6. What resources do I have available (people, money, or otherwise) that might help me overcome the challenges that I've identified?

"We are all experts in our own little niches."
Alex Trebek

CHAPTER II: BECOME A KNOWN ENTITY

"It's what you do that makes you who you are and how you project that to others that makes you memorable."

Dan Schawbel

In addition to having pertinent information or a story to tell that others want to hear about and read, you must "brand" yourself in order to become a known entity. People must know who you are and what you do before they will buy what you produce.

To make sure that you create "buzz" about yourself and your products, you must strive to develop an author platform made up of many different elements of exposure. This concept is crucial for you to successfully generate primary and residual income streams. Think of authors such as Dr. Stephen Covey, Stephen King, Dr. Phil McGraw, Jack Canfield, J.K. Rowling, Dr. Seuss, and countless others. When you hear those names, what genres, topics, or titles come to mind? These authors have been effective in developing a product line associated with their name through their focus on specific topics or categories of books. These writers have also became household names by writing articles, appearing in the media and at events, speaking, and generating name recognition for their titles or themselves. The result is that they have ultimately generated significant streams of revenue from their written and spoken words. In some cases, their books were initially secondary to their careers. Later these became the thing for which they were primarily known because so many people saw or heard them and wanted more information from them in the form of books, articles and other publications.

You are already on your way to branding yourself once you publish a book. Just by taking that step, you become a perceived expert or celebrity to some people. That is because many people say, "One day I'm going to write a book," but only a small percentage of the population ever does.

Think about how someone normally reacts when you first meet him or her in various settings. He or she may ask you what you do and you share your job title or other personal tidbit of information with the person. Does he or she seem to really care? On the other hand, if you respond, "I am an author," the person's whole demeanor often seems to perk up as she or he focuses on you and says something like, "Oh really, what have you written?"

Once you have someone's attention, you then have an opportunity to give your short 30-second "elevator speech" about your book(s). That introductory content is the personal presentation that networking experts suggest that you rehearse so you can quickly let people know what you do in life. Hopefully, if you do a good job and make it interesting and/or entertaining, you move to the next level in the conversation that ultimately leads to selling copies of your book. Or, it could lead to an invitation to speak at a meeting where you will have other opportunities to sell your books or your other services, such as consulting, for example. This is why you should always carry business cards wherever you go and, if possible have copies of your book in your car, briefcase, or other convenient location.

The key to effectively developing name recognition or branding yourself as noted authors have done is to develop a marketing plan and stick with it. Try doing at least one thing per day to market yourself and/or your products. More work is better and you must be consistent in your efforts to get the word out to others about what you do to others. Look at your calendar. What marketing strategies do you have listed each day? If the answer is none, then you are not likely a successful writer. You can be the best writer or most authoritative person in your topic area. However, if you simply sit in front of your computer and write all the time without letting others know what you are doing, no one will know who you are or the value of your work.

By getting people to recognize your products and associate them with your name and face, you can create a powerful revenue generation mechanism.

DEMONSTRATE CREDIBILITY

As an author or writer, you must continually demonstrate your worth if you expect a dedicated following of readers and sales of your work. In addition to having an engaging writing style or voice, you must also show that you know how to effectively weave words together in order to create a valid and meaningful message or story if you plan to be successful.

If you are a fiction writer, credibility is established through material that demonstrates imagination, creativity, and a sound writing style. If you have multiple books that become successful, you begin to cement your standing in the writing community and people start to anticipate your next work.

If you write non-fiction, you must display the same characteristics as a fiction writer, but you must also show that you have the expertise in your selected topic area to add value for readers. They are not paying for your creative prose or to have you drone on and embellish slight content with words that do not contribute to understanding of information. Instead of providing subjective opinion or conjecture, you must thoroughly research your material and present it in a clear, concise, and accurate manner. Since time is valuable for your readers, find a style of writing that provides a lot of useful information in simple fashion while engaging them mentally. Show them how to apply what they are reading so that they do not miss an important point you make. Also, supplement what you say with references to noted sources in order to validate your content and save readers time in having to search for other resources.

The following are other ways to help demonstrate your credibility:

Enter Writing Contests

There are writing contests all over the country for books of various genres. Conduct an Internet search for "writing or book contests" and enter them to gain recognition and get feedback on your articles and book. You also potentially add an award to your writing résumé.

If you win a book contest, most sponsors provide stick-on labels that can be attached to the cover of your winning books and alert potential customers that the book is an "award winning publication." You can also put an electronic copy of the label on your Website next to your book cover for your Website visitors to see.

Seek Book Reviews

Positive book reviews are endorsements of your books. If you visit Amazon, Barnes & Noble, or other online book sellers, you will see reviews for many of the book listings there. These valuable endorsements are often read by potential buyers to help them determine if a book is worth reading or the investment to buy it. Personally, I will often forego or be hesitant to buy a book that has no reviews. I will certainly pause when there are negative comments about the content.

You can encourage people who buy your book to write a review, but I suggest that you avoid trying to bribe or pay someone to do so. There was a popular eBook author of over a million eBook sales on Amazon who suffered a severe drop in credibility when it was discovered that he had paid to get people to write positive reviews for him. This type of approach to get notoriety and make money is viewed poorly by many people and is likely to come across as a sleazy attempt to sell your book.

Send out advance copies of your books to potential reviewers listed in newspapers and other sources in order to get valued feedback.

Some sites for asking for legitimate reviews include:

- http://www.authormarketingclub.com
- http://www.amazon.com/review/top-reviewers

Arrange Local Media Interviews

To get media interviews, you must first identify local and national newspaper reporters and radio or television personalities that handle your content area. It is fairly easy to do this. If they are working for a print publication, just search the Internet with the phrase "List of news reporters in (your city and state)" or "List of reporters at your local television station)." Often, you will find a listing of news reporters by company, along with their contact information. You can also read your local publications to identify the appropriate contacts and then reach out to them. Approach them through email and/or telephone, or through a personal contact who might know them.

Once you are in touch with a reporter, offer to share your expertise with their readers. Newspaper reporters and on-air personalities for radio and television stations are often looking for material and stories that will fill print space and air time with valuable information for their audience. If you can show how you are an expert local resource, the reporters or personalities might use you on a regular basis. An added plus with on-air media interviews is that their interviews are recorded.

Following an interview, the station will normally provide you with a copy of the interview which you can then place on your Website. You can also send it out as an attachment when communicating with potential clients or other media sources.

Get started in your search for media sources by checking the Internet at sites such as:

- http://www.mediapost.com
- http://www.gebbieinc.com
- http://www.helpareporterout.com

GAIN NAME RECOGNITION

A key to improving your sales is to gain name recognition. Luckily, there is no shortage of ways to have people start to recognize your name and associate it with your chosen book genre and titles. With today's expanding technology methodologies, many of your marketing and publicity efforts can be done while you sit in comfortable clothing as you sip your favorite drink in front of your computer. Other strategies require you to reach out to others and become active by getting in front of people to share your thoughts to generate an audience for your works.

If you look at some of the books in the Resources section of this book, you will find hundreds of strategies for getting the word out about your books and what you do.
Some simple marketing strategies that you might employ right away include the following:

Find Ways to Stay in the Forefront

What makes you different or unique in the mind of others? Make a list of these things. Ask friends and peers what they believe you are good at or ways in which you are memorable. Use this information to help you focus your talents when writing without getting pulled away from what you are good at doing. An old country adage sums up this concept... "Go home with the one that brung ya!" In other words, stick with what is important and do not get distracted by other less meaningful things. Trying to be all things to all people is a way of becoming easily forgettable and for you to dilute your strengths or lose focus and enthusiasm.

Once you identify where you will place your efforts and have developed a tangible book or product, find ways to put yourself in front of people so that you can share your work(s). By ensuring that people hear or see you or experience your materials in some form on a regular basis you help ensure that they will remember and relate to you.

Reinforce or Remind

Use personal contacts, your writing, and technology to gain a foothold and stand out from all the other authors and books on the market. In a world where people are overwhelmed by information, you need to be unique and memorable in some way. Finding a particular niche and specializing in only one or two areas or genres is a way of helping accomplish that.

To help do this, when writing your books, consider putting "bounce back opportunities" in the book (*e.g.* at the bottom of pages, in the Introduction and at the end). These might be offers for discounts on multiple copies or a simple partial rebate of purchase price for feedback and comments emailed to you that can then be used on your Website and for marketing. Just don't overdo it and become known as being pushy in trying to encourage opportunities.

Offer them a digital "bribe" that gets you their email address so that you can build a database for future marketing of other books or materials. This might be in the form of a free newsletter, copy of an eBook, white paper, or a report that you have generated on a related topic in exchange for feedback or their buying a copy of your book.

The nice part about building market recognition is that as people get to know you and the quality of your work better, they may buy additional or subsequent products and follow you on LinkedIn and

Twitter or "Like You" on Facebook. Such actions may lead to additional contacts and word-of-mouth publicity. The latter is a crucial and cheap way for promoting your books. If you can get people talking positively to others about you and your works (books), the word will spread quickly and sales will increase, especially through use of social media.

Share Links with Other Sites

Contact other sites that share common content or interests and ask if they would like to cross-link or connect to your Website. Provide them with your URL and get theirs so that you can add them to your site. This strengthens your appearance on the Internet. This is because having links to your site can generate more search engine traffic since search engines look for well-connected Websites.

BECOME AN ASSET

If you want to succeed as an author, you will find a way to try some of the following strategies for getting involved with others, sharing your knowledge and expertise and, in the process, growing your own brand.

Volunteer

I often hear people say, "I don't have time to volunteer or serve on a committee." The truth is that nobody who does these things regularly has the time, but they do it anyway. I believe that we make time for what is important to us. If becoming known and selling your books is REALLY important to you; you will find a way to participate in volunteer activities that gain you exposure and build your reputation. It is an important part of your marketing strategy.

There is no shortage of opportunities for you to volunteer locally or nationally. One of the best ways that I have found to share knowledge and expertise, grow my own knowledge and skills, and give back to the community has been to volunteer. By joining organizations and getting actively involved by serving on committees and in leadership roles on boards, I have met some wonderful people, expanded my opportunities, allowing me to promote my books.

You can do likewise by engaging with religious, professional, business, community, and veterans groups through volunteerism and becoming a known entity within your group(s). If you allow people to get to know and trust you, they learn about your capabilities, personality, and expertise. You can then open a dialog with them to promote and sell your books and products. Often they will offer to do so without being asked.

Speak or Train Others

Publishing a book makes you an instant expert or celebrity. Take advantage of that elevated position to get in front of others to share your knowledge, experiences, and skills or to do readings of your book content.

There will be many opportunities where professional organizations are having conferences and need concurrent session speakers or conference workshop facilitators. Often these groups will offer some type of travel or hotel assistance and a free conference registration where you have an opportunity to network and promote your books or sell them in the conference bookstore.

One thing I always have in my speaker agreement is a statement that as part of, or in lieu of, compensation for speaking, I get two six-foot long tables in the rear of the room to display my materials and sell my books. I also specify that I can put flyers on each attendee's chair. These flyers might be an announcement/order form for a new book, a compilation listing with images of all my other books, or other pertinent information about my products or services.

You want people to walk out of any meeting or presentation with materials that have your name and book or product information all over it. That is why I always put my name, website, and contact information at the bottom of every slide I project in a presentation or at the bottom of every handout page.

At the end of the meeting or presentation I mention that I am available as a future resource on the session topic and point out that they have my contact information if they need to contact me in the future. I am often surprised when I get a call or email from someone a year or so after an event looking for my products, services, or wanting to ask me a question.

As a side note, people who pay or are required to attend a training program or presentation often do not appreciate feeling like a captive audience when a presenter or trainer sells his or her wares from the platform. I suggest that you avoid overt references to your book or materials during your presentation unless someone spontaneously asks for more information about them. This is called "selling from the platform" and can really turn off your audience and sponsors. In such cases, give a brief, courteous response and let them know that you will be in the back of the room by your materials following the event and would be happy to talk further "offline." This will help demonstrate your professionalism and likely win you accolades from attendees and your program sponsor.

In many instances, you can parlay your knowledge into money-making opportunities by conducting workshops that teach people what you know and how they can also capitalize from the content. That is what I do. I have enjoyed good success with the content from this book and other materials I have written through the years. In some instances, I target geographic areas of the country or world that I want to visit and then contact professional groups to offer my services as a speaker and facilitator. In addition to potential back-of-the-room sales at these learning events, my travel and associated expenses can be deducted on my income tax return. Check with your tax professional or visit the Internal Revenue Service (IRS) http://www.irs.gov, or whatever agency handles income taxation in your country, to view current travel and expenses publications for details on how you might do likewise.

Another important point related to book sales is that some states require you to collect and submit state sales taxes for sales within their borders. Make sure you investigate and comply with such requirements if you are going to sell books or products at meetings, presentations, or online through your Website.

Look for other opportunities to speak or deliver training to potential customers or people interested in what you have written. One possibility is to contact bookstores in your area or where you will be traveling for business or vacation to see if they will set up a presentation or book reading followed by a book signing. You can also set up such presentations through social or religious groups to which you belong or that you know about.

If you write non-fiction or workplace related topics, other potential audience targets might be business or professional groups, such as:

- Chambers of Commerce.

- Leadership groups.

- Rotary Clubs.

- Writers groups.

- Libraries.

- Schools and colleges with courses related to your topic(s).

- Society of Human Resource Management (SHRM), Organizational Development (OD) and Association for Talent Development (ATD - formerly ASTD) chapters.

- Professional groups that specialize in a particular topic area on which you have written (*e.g.* medical, accounting, banking, building, teaching, sales, customer service, or whatever).

- Book and warehouse stores that sell books (*e.g.* Barnes & Nobles, Costco, Sam's, BJ's Wholesale Club).

If your focus is fiction, consider groups such as:

- Writers groups.
- Active living facilities for seniors.
- Libraries.
- Book clubs.
- Schools and colleges.
- Country clubs.
- Religious groups.
- Book and warehouse stores that sell books (*e.g.* Costco, Sam's, BJ's Wholesale).

The key is to get a number of these presentations or workshops scheduled at the beginning of each year before event calendars for groups fill up.

Deliver Podcasts

Podcasts are short audio presentations on a given topic and delivered through digital media that can be downloaded to a computer or mobile device, such as a smartphone. A great delivery system for such a program is YouTube, where people regularly search for free content on virtually any topic. One of my future marketing initiatives will be to create a series of podcasts based on the content of this, and other books that I have written.

An important thing to remember before putting yourself in the public eye is that people will always be making a judgment about you and your books based on what they see or hear. If you cannot effectively communicate on camera or do not think you project a professional image, I suggest that you either enlist someone else to deliver your message or skip this strategy.

If you are going to video yourself and put it out on the Internet, consider your grooming and dress, the background behind you in the image, and your non-verbal and verbal communication. Have someone who you believe is objective and who can offer some candid and useful feedback to view any video or audio you create before you hit the upload button on YouTube or another sharing site. Otherwise, you could do more damage than good by sending your message out. Unfortunately, many people who publish on these sites overlook this basic premise and the result is a loss of credibility. To get a sense of what I mean, go to YouTube and type in "self-publishing" and then watch a series of the videos you find there. After each, ask yourself:

- What is my reaction to the person's overall appearance related to grooming and dress?

- Did the speaker come across as a good communicator (*e.g.* good eye contact, facing the camera, no nervous habits or verbal fillers like "uh," "you know," "like," or other similar interjections?

- Was the message clear and useful?

- Would I buy the book, ideas, or products?

Now search for the topic or genre of the book you have written or are planning. These people are your competitors. How do you compare?

Conduct Webinars

Webinars, web conferencing, or online courses are seminars conducted using Internet technology. These technologically produced sessions are popular in today's downsized world where organizations and individuals are looking for ways to learn new knowledge and skills without having to travel to formal training programs or auditoriums. Using the Internet also precludes organizations having to pay facilitators or speakers to come to their location.

In webinars, text-based information is combined with audio and/or video content shared simultaneously over a computer. Attendees from anywhere in the world can log on to a designated Website and participate. In some formats, a telephone is employed to share the audio instruction after participants dial in to a designated number and enter the meeting code.

A nice feature of these events is that they can be recorded for replay later or packaged as a product for sale, thus generating residual income in the future. If you have a non-fiction book on which the content is based, you might also create a supplemental workbook that is shared with attendees during the webinar and made available for purchase separately or as part of registration. Participants can take the course at their leisure by logging onto your Website or some other hosting port.

Some of the more popular software companies that provide the technology to deliver webinars and online training programs include:

- GoToMeeting https://www4.gotomeeting.com/
- anymeeting http://www.anymeeting.com/
- ReadyTalk http://www.readytalk.com/products-services/webinars
- webex http://www.webex.com
- Adobe Connect http://www.adobe.com/products/adobeconnect.html

Coach or Mentor

Whether you recognize it or not, you likely have talents that others would like to develop. If nothing else, you have life experiences that others do not, but could benefit from hearing about.

While it is time consuming, volunteering to coach or mentor others often leads to additional contacts and potential customers. It is also a way of giving back and helping others. Not only can this lead to personal satisfaction for you, but also it might spark potential book and product sales as others get to know you better and realize what you do as an author or through your profession.

Over the years, I have gotten training contracts and book sales by simply going to lunch with someone who approached me following one of my presentations or training events. During our lunch conversation, I assist them with resources and answer questions and they find out more about what I do. This interaction has sometimes led to introductions to others who needed my services or wanted my materials.

As with the speaking opportunities I mentioned earlier in this chapter, look for organizations that might have a need for your books or services and get involved with them. While you may not get rich doing this, you are helping people who may buy your book or be a future consumer and those who might share what you do or write with other potential customers.

There are many organizations in need of people to train, coach, and mentor.

A few of the groups that you might consider to volunteer as a coach or mentor include:

- Professional organizations (based on your profession).
- Local high schools and colleges with literary courses.
- Grade schools looking for volunteer readers for their students.
- Libraries with after-school programs.
- Goodwill Industries.
- Salvation Army.
- Local community colleges or career schools that have grants to assist people in job transition.
- Homeless assistance groups.
- Religious help groups.
- Junior Chambers of Commerce (Jaycees).
- Distributive Education Clubs of America (DECA).
- Junior Achievement.
- Boys and Girls Clubs.
- Boy and Girl Scouts.

Use your imagination and ask others for suggestions of where your talents, knowledge, and skills might be useful in helping others grow personally and professionally.

Create Tip or Fact Sheets

If you are a non-fiction writer, develop short 1-2 page sheets of tips or suggestions related to your book topic or area(s) of expertise. Hand these out free or sell (laminated) at seminars and other events.

If you are a fiction writer, consider developing a tip sheet that lists each character and a brief synopsis of their background to help introduce them to readers as they go through your book. These are also useful if someone puts down a book for a period of time and needs a quick refresher on the characters before restarting their reading.

Conduct Original Research

Non-fiction authors, especially those who write business and academic publications, have many opportunities to select research topics of interest to their current and potential readers. Once you have developed your research data, use it to get publicity and exposure through online (blogs, articles, and e-newsletters) and print (e.g. newspapers, newsletters in organizations, journals, brochures, articles, or magazines) resources. Such original content is particularly of interest to organizations and individuals who have a particular interest in the research topic. You can later write about your research content in future articles and publications to earn income and spread the word about yourself and what you have discovered.

Offer Sponsorships

Non-profit, charitable, business, veterans, religious, and other organizations are constantly looking for ways to generate revenue and help their members or the community. To accomplish this, these organizations often hold auctions, craft and talent shows, rummage and garage sales, and many other public functions. Do a search of local newspapers, sign up for organizational newsletters, join these types of groups, search online (under charitable events in your area), author events, or ask friends and relatives in order to locate these types of events.

Once you have identified possible venues, contact the event sponsor or volunteer coordinators and ask if you might have a table for a book signing in exchange for a donation of signed copies of your books for a live and/or silent auction.

JOIN WRITERS GROUPS

If you do an Internet search for phrases like *writers groups, local writers groups, professional writers groups,* or other similar terms that you might think of, you will quickly find sources that you can tap to provide a support network and a resource for writing assistance.

Many local writers groups meet regularly to hear speakers and successful authors who inspire and inform. Members of these groups also often gather to review and critique one another's works.

PLANNING WORKSHEET

Take a few minutes to jot down responses to the following questions on a sheet of paper. Use this as a planning sheet for preparing to get the word out about you, your books, and/or products and services.

1. What knowledge or skills do I have that make me credible as a writer?

2. What are some strategies that will help me become a better known writer locally?

3. What are some strategies that might help make me a better known writer outside my local area?

4. Where might I use my knowledge and skills identified in Question 1 to become better known?

CHAPTER III: PROMOTE YOURSELF

"Without promotion something terrible happens...NOTHING!"

P.T. Barnum

Promotion and marketing are closely related. For purposes of this book, I address promotion as activities that get you, your name/image and your books and products in front of as many people and as often as possible.

Every person you meet and every organization with which you connect has employees and/or customers who might be a potential customer to buy one or more of your books. Always carry business cards and copies of your book on your person and/or in your vehicle. Give copies of your cards to your spouse, significant other, friends, and family members and ask them to pass them on to others when you and your book(s) come up as a topic in conversation.

Do not push in sharing information about yourself and your books. In many instances when you respond to the question, "What do you do?" with "I am an author," the next question someone asks is, "Really, what have you written?" When this happens, respond professionally in a succinct sentence like, "I wrote _____. It's a book about _____." Next ask, do you read that type of book? Follow this with something like, "Oh, by the way, here is my card if I can be of further service or if you would like to get a copy of my book." Make sure you ask for a card from them and ask if they would like to be added to a mailing list to let them know about future books. If they say yes, note it on their card and add them to your database later. If they say no, just tell them that if they would like more information to contact you at the number or email address on your card.

REPRESENT YOUR BOOKS, PRODUCTS, AND SERVICES PROFESSIONALLY

People form an opinion about you and the products and services you represent in seconds and first impressions typically do not change, or at least change slowly. That is why you should never forget that you are always "on stage" when it comes to meeting people. In other words, there is a possibility that you will encounter likely customers and readers each time you step out of your house or office, send an email, or enter something on a social media discussion group. Everything you say and do is up for potential analysis and comment in today's transparent, technology-driven world.

If you fail to present a clean, professional image in your grooming and dress or do not censure your own thoughts and words online, you may send a negative message that can be shared easily with others in a nanosecond. Those negative impressions can damage your reputation and lead to lost sales or business. At the same time, whenever you encounter someone in line while waiting for service at a business or have an opportunity to communicate with someone in writing, you can seize that moment to make a positive impression. Be pleasant, listen actively, and engage in personal conversation to learn about the person and share information about yourself and your book(s) and product(s), if they seem interested. Remember not to push information on them.

Create a Press Release

A press release is typically issued to the media and other promising marketing sources when something newsworthy happens. For example, to announce your book, notify that you have won a book award or that you have met some milestone (*e.g.* you have a high number of book sales, are placed on New York Best Sellers list, or something similar). The purpose of a release is to convince an editor or reporter that something newsworthy has occurred and that she or he should cover it.

Typically, press releases are sent out alone via fax, e-mail, or postal mail. Press releases might also be included in a full media or press kit that is made available about you, your company, your books, or products.

Many examples of how to write a press release can be found online as well as software that you can purchase to assist you. In general a press release includes the following elements:

- Company logo, name, and contact information.
- Words: For Immediate Release.

- Title (e.g. Local Author Jane Howard Reaches 1 Million Sales on Amazon!).
- Body (Succinct description of event).
- For additional information ... contact name and information at bottom.

Examples of press release formats can be found on the Internet by searching "Sample Press Release."

Develop a Press/Media Kit

The purpose of a press or media kit is to provide images, data, and important information about your book(s), product(s), company, and you to members of the media and potential clients.

The importance of a media or press kit should not be underestimated. The information contained in your kit will provide quick information to a reporter or member of the media who might be interested in writing a story or interviewing you. Since media professionals often work on tight deadlines, they will not typically wait for you to assemble the necessary information. If your competitor has a kit, a reporter may opt to bypass you in favor of another subject.

You can print copies of the press kit contents and place them in a nice folder with your company name and logo on the front. You can also put together electronic versions of press materials on your Website and refer media representatives and other people (*e.g.* potential program sponsors or conference coordinators) to them. By placing the materials on your Website, you can expedite getting it into the hands of those who might need or request it and save the cost of printing and shipping the information to them.

A search of the Internet for "Sample Press/Media Kit" will provide more information about this valuable marketing tool.

Network with Others and Share Ideas

In 1929, Hungarian author, Frigyes Karinthy wrote about his theory in which he believed that the people of the world were continuing to become closer together due to ease of access via travel and communication. He suggested that because of the developing global intimacy that it would be possible for someone to contact anyone in the world through 6 (or less) degrees of separation. In other words, you likely know someone, who knows someone, and so on. This is likely more true today than in 1929 due to electronic media and social networks. As an author, you should capitalize on this phenomenon and reach out to others through your network.

As I mentioned earlier, writing is a solitary function. Build and use a network of friends and professional acquaintances to offer advice on and diversion from your writing. Break away at least once a week to get together with friends, peers, other writers, or experts who can help stimulate and recharge your thinking. This might be for breakfast, lunch, or just to grab a cup of coffee and check in with others.

You might also want to sign up to attend local professional meetings at lunch or dinner. Often these events feature a speaker from whom you can learn new ideas or approaches to writing or your profession. You may also get an overview of the latest products and services pertinent to your career field.

Attend Conferences and Professional Development Events

Attend book, publishing, marketing, Internet and other types of professional conferences to expand your knowledge and become known to others. These venues are great places to educate yourself, get new ideas on the profession of writing, identify potential speaking opportunities, or promote/sell your book(s) and product(s).

As I mentioned earlier, registration and related expenses for these events may be tax deductible business expenses. Additionally, as you read related to speaking and training others, you can sometimes parlay your attendance at conferences and other professional events into mini-vacations by exploring the area around the event location. Just make sure that you keep any expenses for such excursions separate from those legitimate business ones that you will claim for your tax filing. Check current IRS regulations or consult a tax professional for guidance on this.

Often, conference sponsors allow attendees to distribute promotional materials and/or sell their books if there is a bookstore or exposition.

Hold Neighborhood Book Signings

If you are like most people, the only neighbors that you likely interact with regularly and who know that you are an author, live next door or across the street from you.

If you live in a sub-division where you have hundreds of neighbors, let them know who you are and what you do. Expand your network by putting up a sign (e.g. Author Book Signing – your name 9am-1pm), table and chair in the front yard and hold a book signing. Anyone passing by will then know that you are an author and many will likely be curious enough to stop to talk to you and look at your products. You may sell a couple books, but more importantly, everyone in the neighborhood learns about you and can provide word-of-mouth advertising at no cost. Chances are that several of these people have contacts in companies and volunteer organizations that might be interested in purchasing copies of your books or having you come in to speak to their group.

Exhibit at Professional Trade Shows

If you have ever attended a professional trade show in your field or for an interest (e.g. hobby, home improvement, boating, etc), you have seen many company representatives promoting their products and services.

In most of these events where I have exhibited, I have rarely seen an author or independent publisher there touting their publications. For that reason, depending on your topic or genre, I suggest that you explore regional or national trade shows that come to your area or within driving distance that could be promotional venues for you. Local shows reduce your overall out-of-pocket expenses. Because of the expense for exhibit booth rental at larger shows, it might be cost prohibitive if you also fly and stay at hotels. Even in those instances, you can still benefit if you exhibit, arrange book signings at local book stores, libraries or other venues and arrange to speak while you are at a trade show. Many of these expositions are attached to professional conferences where they solicit experts to speak. So if you find one that matches your expertise; you can often receive free conference registration (or discounted registration) or a small financial honorarium for speaking. The nice side benefit of attending the conference as well as exhibiting is that you can network with people who might be interested in your books and attend educational seminars to expand your personal and professional knowledge at little or no additional cost.

In all these instances, you can potentially get a tax deduction for all actual conference, exposition and travel related expenses. If the event happens to be in an area you wanted to visit anyhow, it is a win-win. Take the family along and make a min-vacation out of it. Just make sure you comply with tax laws related to legitimate business related expenses.

Go to Book Fairs

Seek out local, regional, national and international book fairs where you can go to network and make important contacts. You can also gather ideas on how other authors are promoting their publications.

If you have multiple books and products and believe that your content is relevant to potential attendees at a specific fair; consider renting booth space to exhibit your wares. If you do this, consider the fact that, depending on size and location, these events can cost hundreds of dollars for space rental. In addition you have to get there, possibly stay overnight, eat and will have additional expenses. Also, you want to project a professional presence, so you'll need some of the marketing materials outlined in this book and possibly tables/chairs. If outside, you likely want a canopy to keep the sun and other elements off you and your products.

In reality, unless you have a really unique topic that fits with attendees, you may not sell a lot of books, but you can use the opportunity to help start word-of-mouth publicity, pass out materials, and learn from others.

As with any other sales opportunity, be prepared with cash for change, receipts (you can buy these at any major office supply store), and a means to accept credit cards. There are several options for the latter available for smartphones and electronic devices. Instead of signing up for a card processing company that charges large fees, consider newer options like:

- Square https://squareup.com/

- Intuit GoPayment http://www.intuit-gopayment.com
- Pay Anywhere http://www.payanywhere.com/
- PayPal Here https://www.paypal.com/us/webapps/mpp/credit-card-reader

Set Up Autograph Events

Contract the managers of local independent and chain bookstores, as well as, the evening event coordinator at the main branch of your local library. Let them know that you are a local author and determine opportunities to come in to do a reading or speak on your topic to their customers/patrons.
In many instances, sponsoring facilities will make posters and flyers to promote the event, post information on their website, bulletin board or monthly calendar, and may even contact local media to announce your event. If they do not do all this, you can handle many of the tasks yourself. The less work that they have to do, the more receptive they might be to allow you to come in.

Bookstores will often order extra copies of your books to have on-hand. Offer to autograph some additional copies to leave behind. Many people appreciate a personalized copy and once signed, the store cannot return the books for a refund.

Unless you are a noted author or subject matter expert, you will not likely sell a lot of books at a bookstore, but any publicity is good exposure.

With libraries, you might offer 10% of sale proceeds or a couple free copies of your book for the library system. The latter is a good way to keep your book in front of potential readers who may want to order a personal copy or as a gift for others. Related to sales, you are more likely to sell more books at a library than at a bookstore.

Submit for Book Awards

Book awards are a great way to gain recognition for yourself and your work and can generate revenue through awards and book sales, and help sell subsidiary rights.

There are hundreds of various book awards available for differing book genres. Do an Internet search to find ones in your area or that interest you and then submit your book for consideration. Each will have its own criteria, so make sure that your book falls into their categories and requirements before submitting. Submission fees are tax deductible as a professional expense if you itemize your taxes in the United States (check regulation in other countries). Also, if you win an award, your travel expenses to go to an award ceremony to receive it are also deductible. In such instances, you might couple your visit with opportunities to speak locally, do book signings, or otherwise promote your book(s) and product(s).

Some book awards for which you might consider submitting are listed here.

- Independent Book Publishers Awards (IBPA) - Benjamin Franklin Book Awards
  http://ibpabenjaminfranklinawards.com/

- USA Book News - International Book Awards
  http://internationalbookawards.com/

- American Booksellers Association - Indies Choice Book Awards - http://www.bookweb.org/btw/awards/ICBA.html

- International Latino Book Awards - http://www.lbff.us/bookawards

- Axiom Business Book Awards - http://axiomawards.com/

- Association for Library Service to Children - Book and Media Awards - http://www.ala.org/alsc/awardsgrants/bookmedia

- Children's Book Council - Children's Choice Book Awards - http://www.cbcbooks.org/ccba/

- National Book Foundation - National Book Awards - http://www.nationalbook.org/nba_process.html

ADVERTISE

As an old adage goes, "It takes money to make money." Look for local and professional publications, events, and Websites where you might advertise your books, products and services.

Online and print opportunities are often available to promote your book(s) and products via advertising.

One way to get the word out about you and your books and products is to barter with others for promotional opportunities. For example, if you have a friend who is coordinating a professional development event for writers, ask if he or she will allow you to put promotional materials on attendees tables or in the back of the room in exchange for a donation of several signed books to use as door prizes for attendees.

If you are a member of a local writers group, you might consider advertising in their member newsletter or placing an advertisement on their Website.

Pay-Per-Click Advertising

If you have a Website or blog, consider using pay-per-click advertising to get potential customers to your site to view and purchase your books and products. In essence, this is done by visiting Bing http://advertise.bingads.microsoft.com or Google Ads http://googleadwords.com to sign up for an advertiser account and paying a monthly fee based on how many times people click on your advertisements found on each search engines on various Websites.

Once you have an account, use their bidding tool to select the key words or terms related to your book(s), or other products that you want to bid in order to attract customers. By paying for these terms, you help ensure that you are positioned higher on search engine pages and that people see your product advertisement first. If you go to your Internet browser (the application at the top of your Internet page that allows you to search for information on the World Wide Web) and type in any product name or organization, you will get a sense of the value of this approach. The advertisements in bold at the top of the page listings are paid advertisers. The ones at the very top of the list have bid the highest amount for the terms you searched. To see how this works, try a search for "Nonfiction Books" and note the terms that are shown in bold in the top listings, followed by a note for "More Sponsors." These are all advertisers who purchased terms related to nonfiction books.

Affiliate Advertising

In another type of pay for advertising, you might approach a Website owner who has a large following of potential customers you would like to attract to place a banner advertisement on that Website. These small rectangular ads are literally hotlinks that when clicked by a Website visitor takes him or her to your Website where he or she can view and/or purchase your books and products.

Another approach to revenue generation on your site comes from letting companies such as GoogleAds, Yahoo, or Bing to pay you by allowing these affiliate advertising companies to place advertisements from their clients on your Website. This type of advertising can generate a steady stream of income for you. Whenever a visitor to your site clicks (or touches) on the advertisements, he or she is transferred to the advertiser's website to view and/or purchase products or services. In exchange for allowing these ads on your site, you get a percentage of the purchase price when something is bought. There are bloggers and authors making thousands of dollars in passive income each month by using this approach. To find out more about how to enroll in affiliate advertising programs, visit:

- Google AdSense - http://www.google.com/adsense

- Yahoo Advertising - http://advertising.yahoo.com/

- Bing Advertising - http://advertise.bingads.microsoft.com/

- eBay Affiliate- http://pages.ebay.com/affiliate/referral.html

- Amazon Associates - https://affiliate-program.amazon.com/

- Commission Junction - http://www.cj.com/form/advertiser

- ClickBank - http://www.clickbank.com/

GET ASSISTANCE

Constantly remind yourself that you are only one person and cannot do everything by yourself. This is especially true if you are writing full-time as a professional while trying to self-publish, promote your books and products, and/or run a business or work for someone else.

Be selective in getting others to help promote your books, products, and services since, by default, they will also be representing you. Build relationships with individuals, business owners, or anyone else you can think of. Just be careful to find professionals who can deliver on what they promise in a timely and professional manner.

Tap Into Your Network

Even if the people you select happen to be friends or family, be ready to cut them loose if they fail to meet obligations or problems arise. Not only do you not have time to deal with such distractions, but you also need to find viable replacements quickly so you can meet your sales and production goals.

Recognize that not all of the services that you require will have to be paid for. Barter to get people to help when you need someone to edit manuscripts and materials, create graphics, distribute business cards or flyers, put up posters in their place of business, or otherwise perform tasks or share information about you and your book(s).

Enlist family members, friends, or anyone else willing to pitch in. For a small price, you might even hire local high school or college students to distribute promotional materials.

Search for Online Resources

Another inexpensive source to find assistance with various tasks is the Internet. For example, the Website Fiverr (http://www.fiverr.com) is a broker for people willing to perform tasks for only five dollars (U.S.). Through the site, you can contract with people in various parts of the world to print and distribute promotional flyers for you, create company logos, book covers, Web banners or other promotional items, key or transcribe materials, or virtually do any other task in a matter of days. The cover for this book and its eBook companion was designed for less than $100.00 by a freelancer off this site.

As with anything you do related to outsourcing, do your due diligence and get recommendations, read articles about the sites, ask for samples, have a written contract and basically protect yourself when using any Internet site that involves money and potential legal content issues.

Other freelance worker sites include the following.

- 5bux.net http://5bux.net/
- 5spot.ca http://5spot.ca/
- Elance.com https://www.elance.com/
- Freelancer.com https://www.freelancer.com/
- People per hour http://www.peopleperhour.com/
- iFreelance http://www.ifreelance.com/
- Logomyway http://www.logomyway.com/
- AGDesign http://www.allgraphicdesign.com/
- 99 Designs http://www.99designs.com

- Freelance http://www.freelance.com/en/
- ProjectforHire https://www.project4hire.com/

Form Alliances with Other Authors and Writers

One way to get assistance is to work smarter by enlisting the assistance of other like-minded people to help promote your book. Partner with other authors and writers to share information about their non-competing books with your contacts and customers. Perhaps, create a "resources" handout to distribute at events you sponsor or coordinate. Similarly, have your associates do the same for you. If you speak or blog, share contact information about other authors and their books or articles that might be of interest to those with whom you come into contact.

Efforts such as these can add value to the information you provide to your contacts and customers and also helps cement stronger alliances with fellow authors and writers.

PLANNING WORKSHEET

Give some thought to ways that you might creatively promote yourself and your books and/or products and search around the Internet on related topics. Take a piece of paper and jot down answers to the following:

1. Where can I send press releases and media kits for maximum exposure?

2. Whom do I know who might help me promote my books and services?

3. What are some likely business sources for promoting my books locally?

4. What Websites should I visit to connect with online advertisers?

5. What are some Websites where I might promote online?

"You can only become truly accomplished at something you love. Don't make money your goal. Instead, pursue the things you love doing, and then do them so well that people can't take their eyes off you."
Maya Angelou

CHAPTER IV: CREATE MARKETING MATERIALS

"Your premium brand had better be delivering something special, or it's not going to get the business."
Warren Buffet

Always have something to leave behind to promote yourself and your materials following a meeting or event. Such materials help remind people who you are and what you do once you are out of sight. These materials can also direct potential customers to the location of additional information and where your books and products can be purchased.

DEVELOP PRINTED MARKETING MATERIALS

While professional marketing materials might require a bit of a financial commitment; they are worth it. That is because they are your public "face" and people often form opinions about you and your books based on their perceptions of you and what you do. Think about how you have seen successful people and organizations promote their products and services. They create "stuff" that tells their story and keeps them in the public eye.

An old marketing research adage called the "Rule of Seven" points out the necessity for people to see or hear something seven times before they will act on it or make a purchase. While that number may not be set in concrete, it does point to the fact that you must get your message out multiple times and in various formats in order to become a memorable entity and have people decide to become your customers.

With new technology, you can produce some of your own products and they might look pretty good if you do not scrimp on the quality of paper and if you do a good job with design. However, if you are not skilled at producing such items and do not have a friend or acquaintance who can do it, you may still want to hire a professional printing company to handle the task.

If you do decide to produce your own materials or blog and need free or inexpensive
stock photos that can be used for various purposes or clipart of drawn characters or images, check out the following sites that are offered as possible sources,

but should not be construed as an endorsement, For information purposes, the graphic artist that I used for the cover of this book, Joleene Naylor, purchased both the hand and gold bar images on it for $4 (U.S.) each, with no additional fees unless I go over 50,000 in book sales, on http://www.canstock.com.

When visiting an image Website, just make sure you read and agree with the terms of use for each site to ensure you do not violate copyright law and that they may be used for your intended purpose. Another important point to consider about using images that you do not own is that you **must read the user agreement** on whatever site you visit to ensure that they do not require a licensing and ongoing royalty fee for using their images and that you agree with conditions. I suggest that you not get involved in ongoing royalty type of arrangements since it cuts into your book profits.

Here are some sites that you might visit to view images. I have not used all these personally and they are provided for information only. I am not recommending these Websites. Always use due diligence.

- http://www.dreamstime.com
- http://www.canstockphoto.com
- http://www.freedigitalphotos.net/
- http://morguefile.com
- http://www.public-domain-image.com
- http://www.dotgovwatch.com
- http://www.everystockphoto.com
- http://www.flickr.com/creativecommons
- http://www.sxc.hu
- www.Pdclipart.com

Some more common promotional materials that you may want to develop include the following.

Professional Business Cards

Depending on how many books you have published, there are two approaches to the idea of creating a professional looking business card. You might use one or both of these strategies explained in this section. No matter which you choose when producing cards, I suggest that you use a quality glossy paper with four-color images produced by a professional printer instead of doing them yourself on a home computer.

There might be times that it is prudent or practical to print your own business cards inexpensively. For example, if you are attending a professional conference or charity event and plan to drop cards into a bowl for free prizes, there is little sense in wasting time and money on higher quality cards.

Since there are so many cheap options for getting cards printed today, cutting costs should not be your prime excuse for creating them yourself. Companies such as Vista Print (http://www.vistaprint.com) will often run specials of 250 cards for less than $10 (U.S.). Upgrading with glossy paper and color adds a reasonably small price increase. They also print other promotional materials at a reasonable cost. All services are arranged online.

Since card production is relatively simple and inexpensive, I suggest you consider getting two different types of business cards printed.

The first card format that you might consider would be designed to promote your books and would include:

- Photo of book cover image.

- Your contact information on it (*e.g.* name, title [author]).
- Mailing address.
- Phone number.
- Email address.
- Website domain where the book can be viewed and ordered.
- Brief synopsis of the book on the reverse side of the card.

A second card option is to create a professional looking personal business card with your portrait along with all the same contact information mentioned for the book card. On the reverse side, you can list books you have written and any additional services that you provide (see Figure 4-1).

Figure 4-1. Sample Front and Back Business Card

Product Brochures

Brochures come in various design formats and color configurations. Consult with professionals you know or ask others to make recommendations for sources to help you create professional looking brochures. If you are involved in business or professional organizations, chances are someone you know is using or providing the services you seek, or can share the name of someone who can assist.

The key to an effective brochure is that it should be professional, colorful, eye-catching, informative, and brief. Include only key aspects about your books and products along with a brief biography. Don't forget to make your Website domain name where people can obtain your materials prominent in several places. Also, ensure that there is contact information for readers to get back to you.

You can get ideas of what others are doing with their brochures by visiting exposition booths and tables at conferences, trade shows, public events, author events, and by visiting printer Websites on the Internet. Find ones that appeal to you or that really grab your attention. Consider mimicking their format and approach to information sharing.

Book/Product Flyers

Single or double-sided sheets of paper or flyers that have information about your books can be very useful as a reminder of products that potential customers view at a trade show, presentation, or other event. By having these forms at attendee locations or on tables with your books or other products, you provide something that people can take away to remind them to visit your Website or order over the telephone. They can also share information about you and your products with others which increases free word-of-mouth advertising.

The content of your flyer can be a photo and excerpt from your book, a description of content with a Table of Contents shown, praise from others for your book, and a brief author biography. You may also want to put a small tear-off order form with contact information at the bottom so that someone can order the book via mail later by sending in a check (or credit cards, if you accept these).

If you have multiple books and products, you can list a variety of them with brief descriptions on a single flyer.

Bookmarks

For people who read printed books, you can provide a "bookmark" as a helpful tool for them to remember where they left off when they close a book. These little markers are typically printed on paper that is approximately 8" X 2" with information printed on both sides. A 14 or 15 point cover stock paper is often used for glossy or matte printing in four-color. You can also just print in colored ink on heavy cover stock paper to cut costs, but this lacks the "pizzazz" to grab people's attention.

Your purpose for using the cards will dictate what you print on them. You might want to promote your company, book, or product, or simply highlight yourself with a list of your publications and services. In any case, consider using a professional photo of yourself, book(s), or product(s) along with text since that attracts attention and helps with the branding that you seek.

If you search "Printed bookmarks" or something similar online, you will discover a myriad of inexpensive resources for printing. Some companies can have these to you in a matter of days once you approve the proof (design layout), which you will receive from a professional printer or designer to approve before it is finalized.

Postcards

Some people would argue that the use of the postal system to mail marketing materials is outdated and no longer a viable option for promoting yourself and your books and products. If that is the case, then why does the postal service handle over 160 billion pieces of mail each year (as stated by the U.S. Postal Service), including a huge percentage of business marketing materials? If you have looked in your own mailbox recently, you have likely found a lot of correspondence from organizations promoting something.

Even as the price of stamps continues to rise each year, sending out postcards with an image of your latest book along with a product summary and contact information on the back is still a valuable marketing strategy. By mailing out your name and book image on a colorful four-color postcard, you potentially help solidify your name recognition and branding for your books and products. Another nice thing about this form of advertising is that your recipients get the message plus, the postal carriers who handle the mail and see the cover image.

For another option, you can locate companies on the Internet to print your cards inexpensively. Extra cards can be printed and given away at conferences and other events.

Incentives/Giveaways

If you have ever been to a professional or trade show exposition, you have seen companies give away promotional incentives in the form of squeezable stress toys, pens, mouse pads, calendars, office tools, and many other incentives emblazoned with their name and contact information on them. People love free stuff and often take it back for display and use in their office or home. Some items even end up on the kitchen refrigerator for years where people view them over and over.

Taking a page from their marketing playbook, you might consider creating some cute and/or functional giveaways based on your book topic or main character. Add your name or book title and your Web domain or phone number on it, and you have a unique memory jogger. For example, if your book relates to customer service, you might have an incentive featuring a smiley face. I use stress reliever squeezable toys in the shape of brains to remind people of my books and training sessions on brain-based learning and creativity. Such items can assist in branding yourself and your book(s).

Like anything else today, if you search the Internet for "trade show incentives or giveaways" you will likely find hundreds of sources for imprinted items. You can also search the phone book in your local area if you prefer to deal with someone nearby.

My opinion is that if you are going to spend money for giveaway items, make them something functional or that convey the theme of what you or your book are about. Ideally, the items should somehow tie to your book topic, its characters, or some other aspect that those who get them will later associate with you and your books. For example, as a customer service author, trainer, and consultant, I often give imprinted ink pens, eco-friendly grocery carry bags, letter openers, rulers, or mouse pads. I put the name of my organization, domain name, and one of my book titles (*e.g. Customer Service Skills for Success*) on the items to remind people of what I do. All of these types of items will likely end up on someone's desk or get carried around by the person for a while, thus reinforcing the connection when he or she sees it. Remember that you are going for branding yourself and your books and services when you use such items.

Magnetic Signs

You have likely seen small business owners driving around with magnetic signs attached to their vehicles. These can be printed fairly cheaply and displayed on your car to promote your books and services. A search for Vista Print (http://www.vistaprint.com) or other websites will provide you with alternative resources. You can add a book cover image, your photo, a promotional statement and/or book title, along with your domain name and contact information, and you become a mobile billboard.

PLANNING WORKSHEET

Before rushing off to create or purchase marketing materials, you should probably do some planning. Use the following questions as a prompt for your thinking. Respond to each on a sheet of paper and then develop an action plan to market yourself, book(s), product(s) and services, or company better.

1. What is my target market for my books, products, or services?

2. What additional marketing materials will I need for my target market?

3. With what marketing materials do I want to start?

4. What are some resources that I can tap to help develop my marketing materials?

5. Where can I get funding for my materials?

6. Once I develop marketing materials, how will I distribute each one? List each
   type individually and your plan for distribution.

*"If your author platform is not well built,
you may lose readers to an inferior product that
was simply easier to find because its platform
was superior to yours."*
Carole Jelen

CHAPTER V: CREATE AN ONLINE PRESENCE

"It's not what you do once in a while; it's what you do day in and day out that makes a difference."
Jenny Craig

Like it or not, the majority of people in business and many others in society use and expect to interact with a computer in their daily life. These numbers will only grow as we move forward and technology further advances and infiltrates our lives. Savvy marketers and professional writers have figured this out and use technology to enhance their image and sell their wares.

DEVELOP A WEBSITE

According to a web server survey conducted by Netcraft (http://www.netcraft.com) in February 2015, there were over 175 million active websites. That number changes daily as more people and businesses strive to establish a presence and competitive edge by posting their information, products, and services on the Internet.

Are you included in those numbers? If not, you are likely missing an opportunity to share what you do with the rest of the world. You are also potentially missing out on sales of your books, products, and services. Having a website and using other technological communication strategies can be the difference in your becoming a successful author or just writing books that few people ever hear of or read.

Web Hosting
Websites used to be very difficult and costly to establish and maintain. Not only did it require knowledge of computer coding (Hypertext Markup Language - HTML), but also it required paying a webmaster to develop and maintain it for an ongoing fee. That has all changed now. You can get website hosting for as little as $5 a month and most website hosting companies today typically provide easy-to-use templates (the way a website looks) and instructions for setting up a basic site. Hosting companies also provide technical support for

customers who buy their domain name from them or transfer a current domain from another hosting company.

Website hosting companies charge various fees and also have differing levels of service and space provided depending on the plans you select with them. I have used WebsiteSource http://www.websitesource.com for over a decade for my current site and several other company sites I have owned. They have a variety of reasonable rates based on your specific needs, provide good online and telephone support, and have templates and other tools that you can access for free. Based on the plan you select, you get website hosting and email addresses. To give an idea of costs, I currently (2015) pay $6.85 a month and among other things, I get:

- Hosting for 10,000 Standard Domains
- 1,000 Mailboxes
- 1,000 Auto Responders

There are many hosting companies online. Be selective and compare. Talk to your friends and others to see what they use. Also, look for recommendations online. Social media can help with this. Once you have done your homework, choose the service that is right for you. Here are some other popular hosting companies:

- http://www.yahoo.com
- http:www.godaddy.com
- http://www.bluehost.com
- http://www.justhost.com

Website Design

When considering website development, it is important to give some thought to exactly what you put on your website in order to reduce the need for constant update or attention once you have the site developed.

Take some time to search other author sites to get an idea of the range of possibilities. Depending on the money you are willing to spend, you can come up with some very creative designs. My website domain is http://www.robertwlucas.com which was developed by a webmaster.

The following are some well-known author/speaker sites that you might benchmark as a model for developing your own. These likely did not come at a cheap price.

- http://alessandra.com
- http://www.stephenking.com
- http://www.pauladeen.com
- http://www.seussville.com
- http://www.jkrowling.com

If you want a more complex site with a variety of features and opportunities for people to search your website or perform more intricate tasks, you will likely need to pay a web developer and/or have a webmaster to maintain it. Be careful in selecting one of these since some professional developing companies will want to charge you thousands of dollars and build in features you really do not need.

Look for less expensive alternatives. If you are fortunate to know someone who can do this, you can keep costs down significantly. One possibility is to approach students at a local college, career, or vocational school who needs to have a project for class and is willing to do the work at a really cheap rate of around $25 or so per hour.

Other alternatives are:

http:///www.fiverr.com

There are also part-time developers who work with computers full-time at a company and have their own start-up operation on the site who will work inexpensively. They often do this in order to develop prototype websites that they can showcase to other clients and show the quality of their work. Depending on their skill level and how well they perform, this could be a win-win for both of you.

I was fortunate to get that type of deal with a webmaster who developed a website for my former online retail operation. The ultimate cost was around $2,000 for a website that one company quoted $20,000-$25,000 to create. I located him through a technical college that trained people with disabilities (which he was). The guy was a quadriplegic and he was amazing. My entire site was designed with voice commands. He wanted to start a website design company as he was graduating from his program at school and used my site as a marketing example of his work once he was finished. We both benefited from the arrangement.

Whatever approach you take to website development, you should visit your site periodically once it is up and running in order to ensure it has not "crashed" or otherwise stopped functioning, is not experiencing technical difficulties, and that it has current information. Among other things, the hotlinks of website names (they appear blue on a computer screen) that you use for visitors to click in the text on your website in order to get directly to another webpage or product, send you an email or perform other functions sometimes break down and do not work as designed. This is frustrating for site visitors and can lead to people going away without returning in the future. You should also update the look of your site occasionally with different images and content to keep it fresh and attract visitors.

Naming Your Website

Before you purchase a domain name or name your website, an important point to consider is that if you name your site after your URL (Uniform Resource Locator or domain name) it will help with your branding. This is because when people think of your site name, they also know your web address. In my case, my website is Robert W. Lucas Enterprises and my domain name is http://www.robertwlucas.com.

Give your selection careful thought because you want to be unique and not have people inadvertently going to a competitor when searching for your site.

Other things to think about in name and domain selection include:

- What is the purpose of the website? Do you want to inform, display, sell, communicate, or a combination of these? As an author, I suggest the latter should be important to you.
- How much money and time do you want to invest? If you are like most authors, you do not have the time, desire, or expertise to get bogged down in the technical aspects of a Website. Also, if you are a budding author, you likely do not have a lot of expendable cash lying around to spend developing and maintaining a site.

- Do you have a company name or book that you want to showcase or will you be the primary focus?

- Is your goal to monetize and sell your site at some point along with your company? If so, you may not want to name it (or your company for that matter) after yourself. That is because someone else will ultimately own your domain name in your name. Should you later decide you want to use that, it will not be available to you.

- Will this be one of a series of websites? Since domain names and hosting plans are so inexpensive, you may want to develop a site for each book that you write.

As you are looking for a site and domain name, it is a good idea to start thinking about what is called search engine optimization (SEO). In a nutshell, this means making your website and web pages more visible to search engines without having to buy advertising or spend extra money to get a higher listing.

One way to start working on SEO before naming or selecting a domain name is to do a Google search for key words that you are considering for the title or domain. To do this, go to Google Keyword Tool (http://www.googlekeywordtool.com) and type in a variety of options for words you may want to use. Check out the number of monthly local and global (worldwide) searches for those terms.

Once you find words or a phrase that you think that you want to use for your site, visit Network Solutions (http:www.networksolutions.com), or other hosting company that offers a domain search tool, and key in variations of the domain you want to use. This will let you know if the name is available for purchase. If it is, you can either buy it there or visit another hosting company of your choice.

By selecting a domain and company name that people are searching for, you improve the potential visits to the site and a higher position on search engine lists.

One more consideration when buying a domain name is whether you want to buy various domain options. There are .com (commercial), .net (network/internet service companies), .org (organization/non-profits), .biz (small business), .info (information/resource sites) and numerous others that you can buy as an ending for your company name. It seems that in recent years, the domain companies continue to come up with new variations to help them generate money and to continue to have a supply of new domains for individuals and companies desiring to set up websites.

What you have to decide is if you want to buy a number of endings to prevent a future author from writing a book with a similar title to yours should you become a best-selling author or have great success. At the least, most people buy the most common domain ending (.com) and many also buy .net and .biz. You do not have to actually use all the domains that you purchase. In effect, you are capturing them to prevent a competitor from coming along later and purchasing a name similar to yours. In such instances, people searching for you or your book(s) might be confused when searching for your company or name and end up on a competitor's website.

Website Content

Since your website will represent you and your books and products online to the world, you should give some serious thought to the type of information that you include on it.

Visitors to your website will often get there by searching for your name, books or products. In other instances, people will come to your site after connecting to it through another website where your name, books, or products are displayed or discussed. For example, if you write articles and post them on one of the many sites that store and distribute the works of writers, someone might link to your site to learn more about you and any services you provide after reading an article that you have written. Another way for people to locate your site might be through a book reference or product website such as Amazon or Barnes & Noble. Whatever their origin and purpose for landing on your site, you want to make sure they are greeted by a professional looking and easily navigated website.

At the least, consider having the following pages on your site menu:
- *Home* page - where everyone lands initially when they key in, click on, or touch your domain name from a search engine.

- *Articles* page - where any articles you have written are displayed by category. These can be selected for reading and printed or downloaded for use in newsletters or training and educational programs. All of these possibilities lead to free advertising for you and your books and products.

- *Biography* or *About (Your Name)* page - that provides information about you and your products and services.

- *Books/Products* page - with a way to have visitors either purchase from an onsite shopping cart or link to a Website where they can purchase (e.g. http://www.amazon.com).

- If you have multiple books (either fiction or non-fiction) on Amazon, consider setting up individual pages for each book with a cover image, Table of Contents, book descriptions or synopsis, and enough information about the book to hook people and make them want to buy the book to read more.

Consider a sample chapter that they can download to preview. You can also include reviews written about the book.

- *Blog(s)* page - with a drop down menu that appears when their cursor is placed over the "Blogs" tab name and displays the name(s) of your blogs that they can click (or touch) to go to those pages.

- *Client List* page - that provides a listing of current and past clients who have used your services, if you do consulting or conduct training programs.

- *Contact Us* page - that has complete contact information including your name, company name, mailing address, phone number, and email address. Do not make it difficult for people to get in touch with you. If you do that, they probably will not try very hard to do so. Also, provide a fill-in-the-blank form that they can complete and click to email requests for information to you directly.

- *Media Kit* - that has copies of press releases about you and your books or products, publicity photos of you and your book covers, and a copy of your current biography. Also include a link to your articles, upcoming events, and books/products pages for ease of access.

- *Program Offerings* page - where any training or educational programs you conduct are listed and described.

- *Site Map* - that provides a comprehensive listing of all pages on the website and hotlinks that visitors can click on (or touch) to get to any of the pages listed.

- *Testimonials or Reviews* - about you and your books and/or services.

- *Upcoming Events* - provides a listing of speeches, conferences, readings, or other events that you will be conducting during the year and that people can come to meet you, hear you talk, and probably purchase your books and products.

ARTICLES

Another way to gain visibility for your book(s), product(s), and gain name recognition is to regularly write articles and get them published on the Internet and in print. In many instances, you might even get paid if you write for blogs or Websites that hire writers to produce their content. What you have to decide is whether you would rather be paid a flat article or per word fee and give up copyright of the work, or create content for your own blog or website and sell pay-per-click advertising while maintaining copyright control over what you produce. This is an individual choice and you should research the benefits of both before deciding.

It is not enough to simply publish a book and expect it to sell. Part of your marketing strategy should contain ways to stay in front of your audience by writing articles that tie to the book theme or content. For example, if you write children's books, you could write articles for parents related to a theme covered in your book. Say you wrote something that addresses bullying. You could write an article for parents and teachers that provides tips on how to prevent bullying and includes the title of your book and where it can be bought your domain name, and contact information. A novel or book about a law enforcement character or the profession could lend itself to an article on home or firearms safety, personal security, safe driving, or some other topic, You may provide a link to your book in your biography at the end of the article.

Be creative and look for any sort of connection that gets your name and book title(s) in front of as many people as possible. For example, if you are scheduled to speak to a professional group, write an article about your presentation or training topic and ask the organization to send it to members and attendees along with the promotional announcement for the event. Also ask that they list it on their Website and insert it into their newsletter, if they have one. This generates advance awareness about you and your topic.

Some online sites do not pay for articles, but list them for newsletter editors, trainers, and others to read and download for use and distribution (while leaving attributions and biographical information attached). Other sites connect directly to newspaper reporters and others looking for printed content for their publications.

Some potential article writing sources include. Some pay for content, while others do not:

- http://www.ezinearticles.com
- http://www.selfgrowth.com
- http://www.avangate.com
- http://www.helpareporterout.com
- http://www.ehow.com
- http://www.hubpages.com
- http://www.squidoo.com
- http://www.examiner.com
- http://www.articlesbase.com
- http://www.writersweekly.com
- http://www.back2college.com
- http://www.stretcher.com/
- http://travelblog.viator.com

BLOG

The World Wide Web (www) is ablaze with bloggers on virtually any topic. Imagine blogs as public bulletin boards where you can post information and others can respond or add comments about what you write.

Blogs are relatively easy to start once you have purchased a Website domain name. You can address any topic you prefer by simply writing a short piece periodically and posting it on a blog.

One nice thing about creating content for a blog is that at some point you can collect all the entries, reformat them, and turn them into a book that you can publish and use to generate revenue.

Create Your Own Blog

There are a variety of versions of software that can be used to set up a new blog Website or you can simply add one to your existing website as a page. Known as blogging software, weblog software, or blogware, the creators of the various types make it fairly easy for you to get started. They also provide step-by-step help on their websites. Most have upgrades available for a fee that allows additional storage space and functionality as your skills and desires as a blogger grow.

One word of caution related top using "free" blog software...rarely is anything free. With the blog industry, free normally means that the company/person owning the sponsoring site sells ads over which you have no control on your blog, there are restrictive policies on how and what you can do on the site, they continually try to upsell you for additional features and other services, security is often lacking on the site, and you may have little overall control over the blog.

Spend some time researching and select something that works for you and with which you are comfortable using. You would be wise to search out some blogs or forums on blogging, ask friends who have blogs and do some research before making a final decision on how you plan to proceed.

Some of the more common blog software include:

- WordPress – http://www.wordpress.com
- Blogger – http://ww.blogger.com
- Squarespace http://www.squarespace.com
- Typepad – http://www.typepad.com

Once you create your blog, you can select the appearance of it and add what are known as "plugins" to the site. These add-ons perform functions such as tracking statistics related to visitor traffic to your blog, blocking spam or unwanted messages, inserting photos, adding advertisements to the blog, and many others.

Guest Blog

In addition to writing articles and tips to post to your own blog, you can also approach other bloggers and offer to provide content as a guest blogger for their sites. Many are happy to accept such offers because it expands the depth of their offerings and gives them a break from having to write as frequently. Additionally, if you are a known expert, it adds credibility to their blog.

In return for your time and efforts in writing material for others, you get more content that you still control and have copyright to, which you can post on your other social media sites. This expands your reach to a larger audience as you are introduced to markets that you may not have reached otherwise and provides another vehicle for promoting your book, products, and company. An added plus is that you build links to your website and blog by connecting with others, thus increasing visibility on search engines.

Some sources to find other blogs include:

- http://www.myguestblog.com
- http://www.bloggerlinkup.com
- http://www.technorati.com/blogs

Monetize Your Blog

You can make money and generate revenue from your blog by setting up an account with one or more of many online advertisers such as GoogleAdsense, Amazon Associates, or eBay Affiliates. Search the Internet to learn more about these sources.

You can earn money from advertisements placed on your blog in a number of ways:

-**Pay-per-click ads.** You get paid by the advertiser each time someone clicks on a posted advertisement.

-**Pay-per-action ads.** Each time someone clicks on an advertisement and performs an action such as making a purchase or requesting information, you get paid.

-**Pay-per-impression ads.** Each time an advertisement shows up on your blog, you get paid by the advertiser.

Once you develop a good following of visitors to your blog, you might also offer direct advertising for a fee, which you determine. You can contact individuals, companies, or organizations that have products or services related to your blog content and offer to post their advertisements that you upload to your blog. They pay either a flat rate or periodic fee for the exposure you provide to your readers.

A colleague of mine, Zenee Miller, used this monetizing approach and sold her blog for $60,000! (see *Training on the Go, Monetizing Your Blog* http://www.trainingonthego.com or http://www.zeneemiller.com) to learn how she did it. As an IT (technical software) trainer, Zenee is a fountain of information on search engine optimization and often conducts workshops, gives presentations to writer and publisher groups, and consults with individuals and companies at reasonable rates.

SOCIAL MEDIA

A lot has been written about social media and its value in promoting individuals, businesses, and products. Obviously there is a learning curve with all forms of technology; however, if you are selective about what works best for you, you can ease into the world of social connection.

Take a bit of time to explore each of the more prominent sites used by authors, read some articles or eBook on them, and then choose one or two as vehicles to get the word out to the world about you and what you do. The key is not to tackle all social media types at once or you will likely become confused, frustrated, and give up on all of them. Whichever you choose, be sure to link them together so that what you share on one technology platform also appears on the others and you do not have to duplicate work.

Some of the most popular sites for authors include:

- **LinkedIn** (http://www.linkedin.com) is an electronic networking tool with millions of members. To learn more about the site, either do a Google search for "What is LinkedIn?" or visit the LinkedIn website and sign up for an account.

- **Facebook** (http://www.facebook.com) is a social networking platform that started as a way for college students at Harvard University to communicate with one another and expanded to its current size of over one billion worldwide users over the age of thirteen. Once you set up a free account and personal profile, you can begin adding "friends" and can also create a business page to highlight your books and professional efforts.

  Over fifty percent of Facebook users are now accessing the Website through mobile devices such as their smart-phones. Imagine the potential free markets for your books and products.

- **Twitter** (http://www.twitter.com) is an information network where over one hundred million active users sent over 250 million tweets (short messages of 140 words or less) daily around the world in 2012.
Individuals share what they are experiencing instantly. In order to stimulate interest in a new product, a publisher might share real-time information or comments such as, "The new eBook we published on Amazon sells over five hundred copies a day." (If you use this promotional strategy, be sure that the information that you share is accurate so you are not caught fabricating your sales volume).

  You might also use the platform to simply "listen" to others or read their tweets to try to identify trends that might be the subject of a book or article.

- **Pinterest** (http://pinterest.com) is basically a free electronic corkboard where people pin or display images that they want others to see. This format is perfect for sharing your book images after you set up an account.

You can create a Pin Board and gather your book images from sites where they appear and can be purchased (*e.g.* your Website, Barnes & Noble, or Amazon) since Pinterest will link back to the original source of the image(s), thus providing opportunity for viewers to examine and purchase the book.

Another nice feature of Pinterest is that you can link to your Twitter and Facebook accounts and share news pins with those groups as well. You can also add a Pin It button on your web browser so that you can pin images that you come across as you surf the Internet doing research.

As a blogger, you can also pin any images you include with your posts to Pinterest along with the link to the article and blog. This can help increase traffic to what you publish.

The nice thing about all these social media options is that they are free and they go out to the entire World Wide Web that includes billions of users!

SIGNATURE LINE ON EMAIL MESSAGES

A simple way to help market your books is to add a signature line that includes a reference to your books at the end of every email that you send. By including all your contact information and a listing of your books, you make it simple for someone to access or share this information with a simple click of the computer mouse, or touch on one of the screen tiles with the latest Microsoft® software.

Here is an example of how I often sign my professional email messages:

Best Wishes,
Bob Lucas, BS, MA, MA, CPLP
P.O. Box 180487
Casselberry, FL 32718-0487 USA
PH: (407) 695-5535

For customized training programs for you and your business check out: www.robertwlucas.com

For Customer service help:
www.customerserviceskillsbook.com/wordpress
My books: *Please Every Customer: Delivering Stellar Customer*

Service Across Cultures; Customer Service Skills for Success; How to Be a Great Call Center Representative

For Creative training help: www.thecreativetrainer.com/wordpress
My books: *Energize Your Training: Creative Techniques; Workshop Essentials; People Strategies for Trainers; The Big Book of Flip Charts; Engaging the Brain for Learning; Training Skills for Supervisors*

For Communication, Coaching, and Relationships:
My books: *Communicating One-to-One; Coaching Skills: A Guide for Supervisors; Effective Interpersonal Relationships*

For Non-Fiction Writing help: www.robertwlucas.com/wordpress

Like me: www.facebook.com/robertwlucasenterprises

PLANNING WORKSHEET

Online opportunities for marketing abound. On a sheet of paper, list strategies for incorporating the ones that you will realistically use.

1. What online sources are you currently aware of? Which ones are you using?

2. What online resources are available that you would like to learn to use right away? Be realistic about the time commitments required to learn and master each.

3. What resources are available to help you learn and implement the online resources that you have identified as potential promotional vehicles?

CHAPTER VI: DEVELOP PRODUCTS

"If someone likes you, they'll buy what you're selling, whether or not they need it."
Gene Simmons

More products mean more potential income. Depending on the type of books you write and what you decide to sell, you can develop a residual income stream based on products that you sell. These might be marketed on your Website or someone else's, in the back of the room if you do training and presentations, at book readings or signings, or perhaps in stores, or online on sites such as Amazon or eBay.

WRITE ARTICLES

In addition to writing for exposure, branding, or to gain name recognition, you can also generate revenue from works that you create. You can do this by researching websites online that pay writers to compose a variety of materials, such as short stories, "how to" and self-help articles, blog pieces, and advertising or corporate communication text.

Article payment prices range from a scale-based on per-word, per-project or per-article fees. Some writers do nothing but for hire works and make fairly consistent money. If that works for you, then explore the option by searching for pay for writing websites and check out their requirements and pay scale.

As you read earlier, creating your own blog and getting advertisers may be a more lucrative option to selling your works for hire. That is unless getting locked into a set routine with the added responsibility of maintaining a blog does not appeal to you or fit into your schedule. At least with pay-per-piece work, you can do it when and where you like.

WRITE AN EBOOK

Here's a radical idea for you – write an eBook and give it away! Why do this, you might ask? The answer is fairly simple. If your goal is to build name recognition and make more money from writing, then you can use the free eBook to generate word-of-mouth advertising to get people to visit your Website or blog or to attend workshops and presentations you conduct. Additionally, if you provide consulting services, you may generate business contracts once people hear about you through the free book.

The idea about eBooks is that they can range from 20 to 200 pages depending on what you want to communicate to readers. You can create smaller books of 50 to 75 pages in as little as a month on a given topic. For comparison, the first edition (approximately 80 pages) of the book that you are reading took me approximately 4 or 5 weeks to write and publish as an eBook last year. I worked on it an average of six to eight hours a day, six days a week.

Once you create you book, you might offer it free when you do presentations, on your blog, or in email blasts to current and potential clients. You could also announce the free offer on your social media sites or send it out in a tweet, to the news media in a news release, or to others bloggers who can help spread the word. Get creative. Send a release to everyone on your mailing list and ask them to share information about a free copy with everyone on their mailing list. This creative idea illustrates the concept made popular a number of years back called six degrees of separation, where it is said that anyone is only six people away from anyone he or she would like to meet through a "friend of a friend" concept. If this is true, at some point someone famous is likely to hear about your strategy and book and it could really spread. For example, what is the sixth person is Oprah or some other well-connected person…day the First Lady or the President. Don't laugh; stranger things have happened. The point is that your potential is unlimited if you really put effort into distribution of the book.

Other strategies for possible distribution include giving it for free:

- To encourage people to register for an educational event that you are facilitating.
- In exchange for someone signing up early for your newsletter or to join your email distribution list.

- As a bonus for signing up early for a workshop you are promoting.

- To build buzz about another book you have written.

- As a donation for a silent auction.

- As a bonus when someone purchases another product or book you have.

- To high school principals or college professors for distribution to their students.

- As a prize in a drawing at an event.

A nice secondary result of this give-away strategy is that more people might actually start to visit Amazon or other sites where you have it listed. Once there, they may buy printed copies of the book or purchase an eBook. If someone received a free offer, he or she may still find some other items on the site.

Make sure that you take the opportunity to put one or two book/product order forms, an author biography, description of your company products and services, and links to any Website and blog that you have. Your contact information should be included in the front of every book and at the end to make it easy to locate.

One important thing to remember when writing your eBook: do not make it a self-promoting advertisement for yourself or products and services. Readers do not like that and you will garner horrible reviews that could destroy your efforts to positively brand yourself.

CREATE COMPLEMENTARY PRODUCTS

In addition to generating more awareness about you, your books, products, and
your company, develop supplemental products that complement and support what you have written as a means of generating more residual or passive income.

It does not matter whether you have written fiction or non-fiction books, look for ways to build an income stream by developing products that tie to the theme or topic of your book(s). If you focus exclusively on one genre or topic, this is easy to do. Multiple areas of specialty add a bit of challenge, but actually open up new avenues of opportunity.

Fiction Book Products

The fiction genre covers many areas, including children's materials, novels, short stories, historical fiction, novellas, poetry, romance, mystery, science fiction, or westerns. Each has its following of dedicated readers who often find an author they enjoy and cannot wait for their next book to be published.

If a movie is adapted from your book content, that might be even better …if the film makers are true to the story line and do not deviate too far astray. Think Harry Potter, ET, Twilight, Lord of the Rings, and others that have generated an entire line of follow-up products that add to the book authors' substantial wealth. In many cases, theme parks areas have been developed around characters and plots (*e.g.* Jaws, E.T., Harry Potter, Peter Pan, and Transformers).

If this is your writing specialty area, be creative and look to see what is being used to promote the books of mega-star writers. Consider products with memorable quotes or images of characters on them, such as:

- Shirts.
- Mugs.
- Mouse pads.
- Writing pads or notebooks.
- Hats or baseball caps.
- Environmentally-friendly bags.
- Lunch boxes.
- Toys.
- Audio products (*e.g.* MP3 or CD) that are readings of the book content.
- Buttons with clever sayings or quotes.

Non-Fiction Book Products

Travel, textbooks, history, journals, documentaries, essays, photo journals, technical manuals, business skills, and how to books are just some possible categories for non-fiction authors. If this is your genre, consider some of the following add-on products that complement or reinforce book content and can generate additional income.

With this type of book, you can actually produce additional products that add value to the knowledge that readers gain from your books.

- Consider the following as some possible sources of income:

- Audio products (*e.g.* MP3, CD, or Webinars) that contain readings from the book.

- Visual products (*e.g.* DVD or training sessions) of you or someone else teaching a session based on the content.

- Mobile apps for smart-phones and electronic devices based on book content.

- Slide presentations based on book content.

- Cups, hats and shirts with topic themed words, concepts, quotes.

- Workbooks that accompany the books.

- Journals where readers can jot down notes, thoughts, ideas, and action plans based on what they think of while reading the book content.

- Buttons with clever sayings or quotes related to your book topic.

PLANNING WORKSHEET

Conduct some Internet research for ideas on possible products that you might develop based on your book topic and content. Once you identify items and resources, jot down answers to the following questions on a sheet of paper.

1. What are some additional product items that I might develop?

2. What are sources of production for the products that I want to develop? List the product and next to it, resources or possible resources.

3. Where might I get revenue to develop these products?

4. What are likely obstacles in developing these products? How can I overcome these challenges?

CHAPTER VII: WHAT TO DO NEXT

"Twenty years from now you will become more disappointed by the things you didn't do than then the ones you did do."
Mark Twain

Now that you have some ideas for promoting yourself and your book(s) and product(s) it is up to you to take the first step. Go back and look at your responses to questions on each of the Planning Worksheets that appeared at the end of each book chapter. Use those points as an action plan.

Part of your plan should be to create a calendar of activities for branding yourself and your materials. To accomplish this, schedule at least one activity that you will engage in each day to begin your marketing and promotional efforts (e.g. write a blog article, attend a local professional writing event, send out an email blast, or contact potential resources for marketing).

Remember that marketing starts before you write the book and should be part of your initial planning. Always develop a marketing plan for your publications and conduct those activities simultaneously as you do your research and write the book content.

As part of your initiatives start to reach out to your existing network of friends, family and professional associates. Keep in mind that everyone you meet each day is a potential customer for your books and products. Carry business cards wherever you go and make people aware of your plans to write a book or develop and distribute associated products. Get their contact information also, if you think they are truly an interested future customer, then add their information to your marketing database.

Expand your network while expanding your industry knowledge by attending book shows or fairs, writing and publishing conferences or other trade shows that relate to the book writing, production and marketing (e.g. locally or at the national or international level (e.g. Independent Book Publishers Association, Book Expo of America, and Frankfurt Book Fair). These are great venues for making contacts, gathering ideas, brainstorming, and identifying industry resources (e.g. printers, shippers, distributors, graphic artists, agents, and others) that can be of value in your journey to write, publish and sell your wares later.

Another strategy is to offer pre-publication pricing, which can potentially help in gathering names for a mailing list and generate guaranteed income once the book is available (either in print or in electronic format). As you get closer to actual publication and have a cover designed, create a marketing/sales flyer and put information on blogs, websites or in other to which you have access and can share the word of impending publication. Distribute these to potential buyers at professional meetings and in interactions you have with family, friends and other people (e.g. religious events, your children's school settings, family gatherings, or wherever you feel that it might be appropriate.

The bottom line is that no matter how great you think your book or product is; if no one knows about it or can access information on it, you will not sell very many of them.

"The difference between who you are and who you want to be is what you do."
Bill Phillips

 # PERSONAL ACTION PLAN

As part of your efforts to move forward as a successful author, create a list of steps you will take to address each of the following crucial areas for authors in which you feel you need improvement. Instead of looking at it as a New Year Resolution, think "Author Success Resolution."

1.   I will enhance my interpersonal skills in order to better prepare to interact with potential customers, interviewers, contacts, resources and others with whom I come into contact daily. This covers such things as being able to effectively ask open and closed end questions, listen, use and interpret non-verbal body cues and increase my overall communication skills.

_____

_____

_____

2. I will expand my knowledge about the publishing industry and build a network of resources in this area.

_____

_____

_____

3. I will become better at using effective time management skills.

_____

_____

_____

4. I will enhance my knowledge of the Internet, social media and technology (e.g. word processing, graphics, and book design) related to producing and printing a manuscript and books.

_____

_____

_____

5. I will improve my writing skills (e.g. grammar, punctuation, syntax, spelling, and word usage).

6. I will become more of a risk taker rather than waiting for opportunities to occur.

7. I will develop the business skills necessary to be successful in various areas of the writing business (e.g. sales, bookkeeping, business acumen, marketing, and networking).

8.   I will become an asset by getting actively engaged in community affairs, joining professional organizations and becoming a leader and through other means outlined in this book and through other resources.

_____

_____

_____

9.   Other deficit areas I possess?

_____

_____

_____

OTHER BOOKS BY ROBERT W. LUCAS

All of the following books are available at at your favorite book retailer and at http://www.robertwlucas.com.

- *Please Every Customer: Delivering Stellar Customer Service across Cultures*

- *Energize Your Training: Creative Techniques to Engage Learners*

- *Customer Service Skills for Success*

- *Training Workshop Essentials: Designing, Developing and Delivering Learning Events That Get Results*

- *Creative Learning: Activities and Games That REALLY Engage People*

- *The Creative Training Idea Book: Inspired Tips & Techniques for Engaging and Effective Learning*

- *The BIG Book of Flip Charts*

- *How to be a Great Call Center Representative*

"All growth depends upon activity. There is no development physically or intellectually without effort, and effort means work."
Calvin Coolidge

ABOUT ROBERT W. LUCAS ENTERPRISES

Robert W. Lucas Enterprises is an organization dedicated to providing "real world" training and performance solutions to organizations and individuals. Bob Lucas, Principal of the organization, works closely with a network of strategic partners to help clients assess organizational, environmental, and individual human resources needs and challenges. Bob then helps develop or provide appropriate customized strategies and solutions to address identified needs and challenges.

Bob and his associates are highly skilled and knowledgeable professionals who have a wide range of experience in large organizational settings. They are uniquely qualified to provide human resource consultative services and training interventions and stand ready to help provide customized solutions to meet client requirements.

Some of their specialized training topics offered include:

- Train-the-Trainer and Presentation Skills
- Customer Service Skills and Interventions

- Interpersonal Communication (verbal, non-verbal, and listening skills)
- Teambuilding
- Coaching Skills
- Management/Supervisory Skills

For additional information on Robert W. Lucas Enterprises call (407) 695-5535 or visit http://www.robertwlucas.com.

Additionally, if you need free articles and training activities to use in research, newsletters, or professional development resources, visit http://www.robertwlucas.com. You will also find links on the website to Bob Lucas' blogs on creative training, customer service, and non-fiction book writing.

ADDITIONAL RESOURCES

Books and Publications

Baxi, N. K., *The Big Bok of Social media Tips,* Create Space Independent Publishing Platform (2014).

Cabello, F., *Social Media Just for Writers: The Best Online Marketing Tips for Selling Your Books.* CreateSpace Independent Publishing Platform (2013).

Coker, M., *Smashwords Book Marketing Guide: How to Market Any Book for Free* (Free –Kindle) (2011).

Crandall, R., *1001 Ways to Market Your Services: Even if you Hate to Sell,* Contemporary Books, Chicago, IL (1998).

Feeney, Rik, *Writing Books for Fun, Fame, & Fortune,* Richardson Publishing, Altamonte Springs, Fl (2011).

Fry, Patricia, *Promote Your Book: Over 250 Proven, Low-Cost Tips and Techniques for the Enterprising Author,* Allworth Press (2011).

Howard-Johnson, C., *The Frugal Book Promoter: How to get nearly free publicity on your own or by partnering with your publisher (2nd ed)*, CreateSpace Independent Publishing Platform (2011).

IRS Publication 463 (2015) *Travel, Entertainment, Gift, and Car Expenses* (changes yearly).

Kremer, J., *1001 Ways to Market Your Books,* Open Horizons, Taos, NM (2008).

Kukral, J., *The Ultimate Digital Book Promotion Handbook – The Author's Guide to Finding Places to Promote Your Book Online,* (Kindle) (2012).

Levinson, J.C., Frishman, R., Larsen, M., and Hancock, D.L., *Guerilla Marketing for Writers: 100 No-Cost, Low-Cost Weapons for Selling Your Work. 2nd Ed.* Morgan James Publishing, Garden City, N.Y., (2010).

Lizotte, K., *The Expert's Edge: Become the Go-To Authority People Turn to Every Time.* McGraw-Hill Education, Burr Ridge, Il. (2007).

Maroevich, B., *EBOOK Publishing Guide: How to Write an Ebook and Publish It Online In Less Than 7 Days!* (Kindle) (2012).

Miller, P.Z., *Top Tips for How to Market Your Book on Amazon and Facebook: Action Steps You Can Do Immediately Whether You Are Traditionally Published or Self-Published.* (Kindle) (2012).

Pinskey, R., *101 Ways to Promote Yourself: Tricks of the Trade for Taking Charge of Your Own Success.* Avon Books (1999).

Poynter, D., *How to Write, Print and Sell Your Own Book. Para Publishing Vol 2.*, Santa Barbara, CA (2009).

Ross, M. & Collier, S., *The Complete Guide to Self-Publishing (5th Ed).* Writer's Digest Books, Cincinnati, OH (2010).

Walters, L., *1001 Ways to Make More Money as a Speaker, Consultant or Trainer,* McGraw-Hill, NY (2004).

NOTE: On any given day, go to http://www.amazon.com/books and search for books on topics like book marketing, author platform, book promotion, book sales or related topics and you will find numerous free Kindle books being offered.

Organizations and Associations

Florida Authors and Publishers Association
http://www.floridapublishersassociation.com offers authors, book publishers, self-publishers, publishing industry friends, publishing vendors, and students engaged in writing curriculums an opportunity for professional development and networking; provides its members with support, and is a clearinghouse for up-to-date book publishing information. Membership is open to anyone in the industry or interested in it.

Florida Writers Association
http://www.floridawriters.net is a professional networking site dedicated to "writers helping writers." Members can access other members, articles, conferences, and other pertinent resources to help hone their knowledge and skills about writing for fun and profit.

Independent Book Publishers Association
http://www.ibpa-online.org/ is the largest association of independent publishers in the United States and assists members to market their books to libraries, bookstores, and other sources. In addition, the organization is an advocate for members in the publishing industry and provides educational opportunities to assist publishers in handling various elements of their business.

Writer's Digest
http://www.writersdigest.com was established in 1920 as a resource for freelance fiction and non-fiction writers who want to get their works published. The publication provides up-to-date strategies to help aspiring and established writers and authors navigate the process of becoming published. Articles are written by established authors and writing professionals who provide timely advice to assist those engaged in the writing profession.

NOTE: Do an Internet search for writer, author and publisher groups or associations in your local area to find resources that you have nearby. Start attending meetings and join those organizations to expand your personal network and sphere of influence. This is part of you author platform that you read about earlier.

REQUEST FOR REVIEWS

As an author, you can appreciate the importance of feedback. Likewise, I will appreciate your visiting Amazon (http://www.amazon.com) and leaving some objective feedback about this book. Your comments will also aid other potential readers in making a decision on whether to purchase a copy of this book.

I have a passion for what I do and hope that comes across in my writing. My goal in writing this book, and others, is to provide you with information and ideas that can enhance your potential for success as an author and/or self-publisher. I hope that the content of this book prompted some thoughts on your part and that you will put some real effort into promoting your book and generating residual and passive income in coming months.

If you have specific suggestions related to the content or format of the book, please email your thoughts to me at info@robertwlucas.com with a subject line of *"Feedback on Make Money Writing Books."* Provide me a name and complete mailing address in the text area and I will send you a copy of the first edition of my booklet *Communicating One-To-One: Making the Most of Interpersonal Relationships.*

Thanks for your assistance. If you would like to be added to a mailing list to learn about my other books and ones that I will be publishing in the future, please email me at info@robertwlucas.com with a subject line of "Add to Mailing List."

Please remember to visit my blogs at www.robertwlucas.com and to Like me on Facebook at www.facebook.com/robertwlucasenterprises.

Let me know if I can be of future assistance.
Bob Lucas - http://www.robertwlucas.com

ORDER FORM
Make Money Writing Books

Costs (per copy – U.S. dollars)	Copies Ordered	Sub-Total
1 copy @ $12.95 each	_____	_____
2-10 @ $11.65 each	_____	_____
11-50 @ $10.35 each	_____	_____
51+ @ $ 9.05 each	_____	_____

Recipients in Florida - add applicable: State and local taxes and local taxes

Shipping/Handling

TOTAL _____

Shipping/Handling: 1 copy =$3.95   2-6 copies= $5.95
7 or more and international   = based on weight (call/email before ordering)

Overnight Express and international delivery available at actual cost, plus $5.00.
☐ Check here for express delivery

NOTE: Prices subject to change without notice.

Checks drawn on U.S. Banks in U.S. currency only and U.S. Postal Money Orders accepted.

☐ Check/MO# _____ enclosed

☐ Organizational Invoice (P.O. # _____ enclosed)

Ship To Address (No P.O. Boxes please):
_____
_____

Phone: _____ Email:_____

Robert W. Lucas Enterprises 1555 Pinehurst Drive, Casselberry, FL 32707, USA
PH:+1-(407)695-5535. Email : info@robertwlucas.com

ORDER FORM
Make Money Writing Books

Costs (per copy – U.S. dollars)   Copies Ordered   Sub-Total

1 copy @ $12.95 each   _____   _____

2-10 @ $11.65 each   _____   _____

11-50 @ $10.35 each   _____   _____

51+   @ $ 9.05 each   _____   _____

Recipients in Florida - add applicable: State and local taxes and local taxes

Shipping/Handling

                                       TOTAL   _____

Shipping/Handling: 1 copy =$3.95   2-6 copies= $5.95
7 or more and international = based on weight (call/email before ordering)

Overnight Express and international delivery available at actual cost, plus $5.00.
☐ Check here for express delivery

NOTE: Prices subject to change without notice.

Checks drawn on U.S. Banks in U.S. currency only and U.S. Postal Money Orders accepted.

         ☐ Check/MO# _____ enclosed

Ship To Address (No P.O. Boxes please):

_____

_____

Phone: _____   Email:_____

Robert W. Lucas Enterprises 1555 Pinehurst Drive, Casselberry, FL 32707, USA
PH:+1-(407)695-5535. Email : info@robertwlucas.com

www.ingramcontent.com/pod-product-compliance
Lightning Source LLC
Chambersburg PA
CBHW070759040426
42333CB00060B/1228